THE KOREAN ART OF LIVING WELL

The Eight Keys of Living Meditation for Balance and Transformation

AMARYLLIS

AMARYLLIS

An imprint of Manjul Publishing House Pvt. Ltd.
• C-16, Sector 3, Noida, Uttar Pradesh 201301, India
Website: www.manjulindia.com
Registered Office:
• 2nd Floor, Usha Preet Complex,
42, Malviya Nagar, Bhopal 462 003 - India
Distribution Centres
Ahmedabad, Bengaluru, Chennai, Hyderabad,
Kochi, Kolkata, Mumbai, Noida, Pune

This edition first published in India in 2026 by
Amaryllis – an imprint of Manjul Publishing House Pvt. Ltd.

ISBN 978-93-7317-184-5

Printed and bound in India by Parksons Graphics Pvt. Ltd.

PRAISE FOR THE KOREAN ART OF LIVING WELL

"This beautiful book is more than wisdom – it's an invitation to live with peace, integrity and love. Dr Jenelle Kim shares teachings of timeless principles and simple practices empowering calm, clarity and resilience while opening your heart to deeper connection and purpose. The Korean Art of Living Well *is a gift to the soul."*

Jack Canfield, Coauthor of the *Chicken Soup for the Soul®* series and The Success Principles™

"The wisdom shared by Dr Jenelle Kim flows directly from the heart of the Tao, and from her own deep spiritual practice. In The Korean Art of Living Well, *Dr Kim bridges ancient and modern in a way that feels effortless, grounded and deeply human. She reminds us that meditation isn't about escaping life... it's about awakening fully within it. This book is for anyone seeking to live with more balance, presence and purpose."*

Kevin Ellerton, founder of *Meditation Magazine* and Meditation University

"Dr Jenelle Kim's The Korean Art of Living Well *is a bridge between ancient wisdom and modern living. Through the eight keys of Living Meditation, she shares how to integrate presence, purpose and balance into the fast-paced world we live in. Her teachings beautifully align with what we aim to share at Biohack Yourself Media, helping people optimize their inner and outer worlds to live long and healthy lives with more awareness and vitality."*

Anthony Lolli and TereZa Hakobyan-Lolli, founders of Biohack Yourself Media

"Dr Jenelle Kim bridges the wisdom of the East with the pace and challenges of modern life. In The Korean Art of Living Well, *she doesn't just teach meditation, but shows you how to live it. Her words are a reminder that true healing begins in how we move through each moment and this book is a call to return to the peace that was always within."*

Frank Elaridi, Four-Time Emmy Award Winning Journalist, Author & Energy Healer

Dr Jenelle Kim

THE KOREAN ART OF LIVING WELL

The Eight Keys of Living Meditation for Balance and Transformation

CONTENTS

To my father:

It is my greatest wish to be by your side eternally because next to you nothing in this world is impossible and the ground is never shaky.

Your unwavering love, compassion and power vibrate through the wavelengths of the universe and every life that you touch is enriched with a deeper understanding of what is true in this universe, what is important. Your mere presence grounds those that stand before you because you are the essence of what it means to be human. You bring light to the world, giving hope and direction. At one time, I thought I would never know a more loving being, a more true soul, a more extraordinary spirit, but you taught me that the essence of this spirit exists within each of us, and it is our choice to cultivate it and let it shine through.

The greatest gift I have ever been given was the gift of being your daughter. Through this experience and your unwavering example of what it means to truly be a good person, I have come to understand what it is to be a good mother, wife, sister, friend. You have shown me the road.

I have set my mind and my heart to share all of the principles that you have dedicated your life to sharing with this world, as they were shared with you. I know that without these universal principles this world will never know true humanity, hope, togetherness, compassion and empathy.

Your daughter and ever faithful student,

Jenelle

INTRODUCTION

Most forms of meditation ask us to be still and quiet. We must take time away from our busy lives and forget about our ever–growing to–do lists. However, it's not always easy to take a step back.

Living Meditation® is the opposite of this. It is a form of meditation that is active, dynamic and woven into our everyday lives. It is a form of meditation that helps us to see ourselves, and therefore the world, more clearly.

Living Meditation is a daily practice that uses eight "Keys" as tools to examine every situation we find ourselves in, so that we may become more aware of ourselves, make the correct choices and gain perspective in every circumstance. In this way we are able to engage with life more deeply and discover our place and purpose in the world.

Living Meditation helps us to remain present, aware, grounded and connected so that we may lead a harmonious and balanced life, no matter what is happening around us.

The Heritage of Living Meditation

Living Meditation draws from the great Eastern philosophies of East Asia and Korea, where Taoism took root during the Three Kingdoms period. Tao, in its truest sense, is the natural order of the universe. It is the harmony of yin and yang, the flow of all things. To live in accordance with the Tao is to live with balance, integrity and connection.

As the American-born daughter of a Korean father and an American mother, I learned from an early age the power behind the centuries-old medicine and principles of the Korean art of living well and Living Meditation, derived from the Tao and passed down from my ancestors.

I am honoured to be the first woman in my lineage to serve as the guardian of these ancient teachings. For nine generations, these sacred principles and tools have been passed on – alongside a treasury of herbal medicine, martial arts (Qi Gong), and Eastern philosophy. Now, I am bringing these tools to a wider audience in a way that is practical, accessible, effective and lifechanging.

Unlocking the Eight Keys: Ancient Wisdom to Navigate Modern Life

Most forms of meditation ask us to be still and quiet. They ask us to pause, step away from our responsibilities, and silence the world around us. But how often can we truly remove ourselves from life's chaos and the demands of our ever-growing to-do lists?

Living Meditation is the opposite. It is a form of meditation that is dynamic, active and fully integrated into our everyday life. It teaches us that peace is not something we must escape to find – it is something we can cultivate in the midst of it all.

Living Meditation is a daily practice offering a path to clarity, presence and harmony. Through its eight keys, we are given tools to examine any situation, no matter how challenging, and respond with grounded wisdom, greater perspective and *correct* action. By using these principles, we learn to be more aware of ourselves, to see ourselves more clearly – and therefore see the world more clearly. This awareness and clarity become our strength. In this way we are able to engage with life more deeply and discover our place and purpose in the world.

As we deepen our Living Meditation practice, we naturally begin to move through life with more grace, presence and purpose. We stay connected – even in moments of stress or uncertainty – and that connection allows us to live with balance between our mind, body and spirit. Living Meditation gives us a way of being that is aware, calm, decisive and harmonious. It empowers us to *balance WITH life*.

These benefits do not come overnight – but through consistent practice of the eight keys, you will begin to transform the way you live your life.

Connection: The Core of the Korean Art of Living Well

All things in nature and our surroundings share a connection. Some call this an energy, others a life force. I like to simply call it connectedness. When we begin practising Living Meditation, we become more aware of this connectedness. We start learning more about ourselves, our relationships and our effect on the world around us. Living Meditation offers us a way of being that is aware, calm, decisive and harmonious. It teaches us how to resolve conflict, walk through stress, and accomplish any goal by gaining perspective and creating good habits in our daily life.

All of our struggles – in work, relationships, parenting, friendships, health, money and family – become less challenging. We begin feeling a greater sense of balance between our mind, body and spirit, because we are able to see ourselves, as well as the people and circumstances around us, more clearly by purifying our minds and following through with correct choices and actions, which in turn creates good habits.

Of course, these changes do not come overnight, but by practising the **eight keys of Living Meditation**, you can begin to balance and transform the way you live your life.

THE EIGHT KEYS OF LIVING MEDITATION

Key 1: Know Your True Self

Life presents us with unlimited opportunities to learn about our true selves. Knowing who we truly are puts us on a path to become the greatest version of ourselves.

Key 2: The True-Right-Correct Method

What is *true* is a reflection of our inner state. The *right* decision is what does the best for everyone involved. The *correct* choice to make is a balance between what is right and what is true.

Key 3: Stop Being Drunk on Your Own Thoughts

In Korean, *Doe Chi* means to be "drunk on one's thoughts". We use this phrase to describe those who allow their thoughts and beliefs to limit their view. To practice Living Meditation, we widen our perspective, and then we take accountability for our actions and see our circumstances clearly. Through this we become empowered and able to change our own reality.

Key 4: How Will You Be Remembered?

We are all going to leave a legacy. How significant that legacy is depends on us. When we begin looking for ways to plant seeds of goodness for future generations, we often notice that there are small, everyday opportunities to do so all around us.

Key 5: Seek Connectedness & Honour

To live with honour means to respect others for the role they perform for the good of all. This respect is based on a deep appreciation and underlying love for all living things.

Key 6: Change Your Reality for the Better

We all have the ability to change our realities for better or for worse. When we let our inner world determine our outer reality, we can cultivate a sense of deep peace and strength that carries us through every situation.

Key 7: It Only Takes One Match to Light a Thousand

It only takes one positive action, one person or one thought to ignite a thousand more. However, just as there is night and day, loud and soft, masculine and feminine, yin and yang, there is always positive and negative, which means that just as this principle applies to the positive, it also means that one negative action, person or thought can ignite a thousand more. If we know the impact that even one of our thoughts has, then we can be that much more aware of the fact that **each one of us holds the power** and has the choice in any and every situation to make our lives and the lives of those around us better or not. No moment is unimportant.

Key 8: Be Like Bamboo

There are times to be hard and there are times to be flexible. This is the balance of life. Instead of always being inflexible, be like bamboo: strong but flexible so as not to break, with knowledge, experience and wisdom that softly moves with the rhythm of the Tao – the way of the universe.

The Three Pillars: Mindset, Medicine and Movement

At the heart of the Korean art of living well are three pillars, or what I call the **Three Ms.**

Mindset

Living Meditation is the foundation of the mindset pillar and this is the main focus of this book. Rather than separating meditation from the rest of life, we integrate it into each moment. Whether we are working, parenting, walking or preparing a meal, we can practise being present, aware and aligned with our core values. The eight keys of Living Meditation help us examine our thoughts and behaviours and make conscious, harmonious decisions in real time. We learn to gain perspective moment by moment with a new sense of clarity and awareness. Often, if we can change our perspective, we can change our life.

Medicine

As a doctor and herbal formulator in my lineage, and founder of JBK Wellness Labs – my contract manufacturing labs where we create effective and innovative beauty and wellness products for renowned brands across the globe – I have seen firsthand how natural medicine nourishes and restores the body. Traditional medicine is not only a remedy, it's also a way of living in harmony with our mind, body and nature. It teaches us to listen to our bodies, identify imbalances and support our wellbeing through herbs, nutrition, breath and movement. When we make health a daily intention, we empower ourselves to live more fully.

Movement

Movement is Medicine. Movement is energy (*qi* – vital energy) in action. By incorporating specific powerful movements and techniques that are combined with breath and have been handed down by our ancient teachers and masters for centuries, we can balance and rejuvenate our mind and body, remove stagnation, gain energy and maintain optimal health, beauty and longevity. We learn to feel the natural energy that exists within us and connects us to all living things and with nature. Through the benefits of movement, we become more aware of how our actions affect our minds and bodies and those of the people around us, and we learn to move with the flow of the universe. Remember, when our bodies function properly and are in flow, we can attain a life of balance and overall wellness; we can live to our fullest.

In my teachings, movement comes through martial arts (Qi Gong) and breathwork. However, it also comes through the way we walk, the way we breathe, the way we carry ourselves through each day. Movement reminds us that we are connected – to ourselves, to nature and to the universe.

These Three Ms – **Mindset, Medicine and Movement** – are not separate practices. They are deeply interwoven, born from the same root: the Tao. When we live in accordance with the Tao, we begin to live well. We begin to truly understand ourselves and our place in the world. This is the secret to attaining optimal health, longevity and beauty.

This is the Korean art of living well.

How to Apply the Secret Teachings in Daily Life: The Three As

In the Korean art of living well, we do not seek to escape from life – we seek to live in harmony with it. This is the essence of Living Meditation, which reminds us that balance is not found in extremes but in the simple, consistent practices we embody every day. It teaches us that balance is not something we find in isolation or stillness alone. True balance is cultivated in the midst of our daily responsibilities, emotions, relationships and choices.

This is where **the Three As** come in – **Acknowledge, Assess, Act** – a simple yet profound framework and guiding compass for integrating the Three Ms of Living Meditation – Movement, Medicine and Mindset — into practical, daily use.

Whether you are navigating a moment of stress, experiencing emotional overwhelm or seeking clarity in a difficult situation, the Three As offer a clear, grounded approach for transformation. They bring ancient wisdom into modern life in a way that is practical, embodied and sustainable.

Acknowledge

Pause. Breathe. In a world that pulls us outward, this is your invitation to turn inward.

How do you feel – physically, mentally, emotionally? Is your body energized or tired? Is your mind scattered or focused? Are you holding tension or flowing freely?

This step is about honest presence – without judgement, without resistance. When we acknowledge what *is*, we become grounded in truth. Only from this place can real change begin.

Assess

Once we acknowledge our inner state, we step into observation. We ask:

What is out of balance? What patterns are repeating? What are the subtle signals – within our body, our mind, our relationships – that we may have been ignoring?

This is where we apply the eight keys of Living Meditation. These ancient principles act as a compass, helping us examine any situation through the lens of clarity, compassion, and awareness. They teach us how to perceive beyond our immediate emotions, how to listen deeply and how to respond from a place of centered wisdom.

However, it is important to understand that *assessment is not the same as over-analysis*. There is a fine line between mindful observation and getting stuck in the spiral of blame – whether blaming ourselves, others or our circumstances. When we remain in this state for too long, we begin to stagnate. Energetically, mentally, emotionally, we become trapped. And the deeper we fall into this hole, the harder it becomes to climb out.

This is why we must keep moving forward.

Act

Awareness is powerful, but it is action that creates change and transformation.

Once you've acknowledged your state and assessed your internal and external landscape, you are ready to move forward. At this moment, it is essential to take the first step – no matter how small. This initial movement shifts your energy, breaks through stagnation and sets everything into motion.

After assessing your options in any given situation, do not wait for the "perfect" answer. Waiting too long, overthinking or fearing imperfection can keep us paralyzed. Instead, allow your insights to guide you toward one aligned action – and take it with intention.

This is how we activate the wisdom of the Three Ms:

- Through Movement, we shift our energy physically and energetically.

- Through Medicine, we nourish ourselves with what is truly supportive.

- Through Mindset, we stay rooted in the eight keys, gaining clarity and alignment.

Taking that first step initiates a powerful process – it places you on a path toward the outcome you desire. From there, the goal is to continue expanding your mind and gaining perspective, so that when life calls you to pivot or redirect, you can do so with clarity, not confusion.

True wisdom lies in the ability to act with purpose, adapt with awareness and continue forward with trust in the process. Whatever the action, the most important part is this: *You do not remain still. You do not remain stuck.*

Movement is medicine, it brings life. Stagnation brings suffering. Action is transformation.

The Meeting Point of Mindfulness & The Tao

Taoism was introduced to Korea from China during the Three Kingdoms period (AD 220–280) and remains as a significant element of Korean thought today. In Chinese philosophy, Tao is the absolute principle underlying the universe, combining within itself the principles of yin and yang and signifying the way, or code of behaviour, that is in harmony with the natural order.

According to the American Psychological Association (APA.org, 2012), mindfulness is: "… a moment-to-moment awareness of one's experience without judgment." Or as Jon Kabat Zinn puts it, mindfulness is "The awareness that arises from paying attention, on purpose, in the present moment and non-judgmentally."[1]

When we combine this awareness with the wisdom of the Tao, we create a powerful way of life – a new lens through which to see the world. This is Living Meditation.

1 Kabat-Zinn, J, *Wherever You Go, There You Are: Mindfulness Meditation in Everyday Life*, Hyperion, New York, 1994

The Power of Cultivating the Energy of Nature

East Asian masters, doctors, philosophers and martial artists over the centuries have taught correct ways to enhance wellness, increase vitality and achieve balance, calm and harmony. By balancing mind, body and spirit, and connecting with the limitless reserves of natural energy around them, they found that they could place themselves beyond the persistent negative influences in life, such as stress and conflict. In our modern world, this wisdom can be applied to remedy tension, anxiety, depression, discord, emptiness and exhaustion.

Living Meditation takes its cues from the natural world and uses the energy of nature to permeate the body, mind and heart. In each chapter of this book, I will share a story that draws on images of trees and mountains, rivers and sunlight. These stories are based on my father's learnings from his time as a young monk in Korea.

The Seven-Year-Old in the Mountains of Korea

As a boy of seven, my father had to leave his family to live in the mountains of Korea and learn from a master. Training young boys in intellectual and philosophical pursuits, martial arts and artistic and cultural practices was a longstanding Korean tradition.

Being accepted by the master as a student was the first challenge. Not knowing what to do, my father spent the first several days waiting outside the entrance to the master's *Am Ja* (a cave or practice/living space), watching him come and go. Master Borion ignored his every word and gave not the slightest sign that he even saw him there. But my father was determined to become his student, so he set up camp on the master's doorstep. Living on roots, berries and other foraged foods, he waited for acceptance – or at least some word of encouragement. Nothing came. My father watched Master Borion go in and out every day, then began to follow him on short trips to get water or food. Nothing happened.

A voice within my father's mind tried to persuade him that his plan was futile, but he refused to listen. He believed that he was meant to be Master Borion's student, and nothing would dissuade him.

Finally, after five months, the master quietly motioned to my father that he was to enter.

That started a relationship that was priceless to my father. Master Borion opened the door to the greatest knowledge passed down through the centuries and made it possible for my father to cultivate the "good seeds" of harmony and peace to leave behind for others. You see, in those early months, the master took in everything about my father. He heard all and saw all. But only after the master knew that my father could learn and absorb what he needed to learn and stay on the straight course did he open the door and let him in.

My father's education in the mountains lasted seven years. Upon reaching enlightenment at the age of fourteen, he was given the name *He Kwang*. It is translated as "Bright Sun", and this name perfectly embodies the essence of my father.

This is one of the few remaining photos of him from that time.

My father was my greatest mentor. He was a man of deep compassion, empathy, wisdom and perspective. I lost my father when I was 33 years of age, but he has never stopped teaching me. The lessons he taught me while he was physically here have reached me even deeper than they ever did while he was on this earth.

My Intention and Duty

This is my calling and my duty – to open this door for you. To pass forward the eight keys, the secret teachings I was entrusted with. To guide you in the Korean art of living well.

For centuries, only a select few individuals have been able to learn directly from a master. Such selectivity also applied to the mysteries of the healing arts that were my heritage. Now, as we move into a new era where the highest ideals and practices of East and West are flowing together into a greater whole, I believe that the time has come to share these teachings with a wider audience. My intention, and my heart's deepest desire, is to bring the healing influence of Living Meditation and the Korean art of living well to people and families everywhere so that we can all enjoy increased wellbeing and greater connection as part of our daily lives.

This is not simply a book to read – it is a path to walk, a set of practices to live, a way to return to your true self.

Let us begin.

How to Use This Book

The eight keys form the heart of Living Meditation, so each chapter in this book presents one of those keys. Each chapter also centres on a story about my father's time in the mountains, learning from Master Borion. I invite you to imagine yourself in the place of my father: picture yourself as the student, so that you move from passive listener to active participant. This way, you can internalize these principles and absorb them into your own patterns of thought and action.

Traditionally, only a select few individuals have been able to learn directly from a master. Such selectivity also applied to the mysteries of the healing arts that were my heritage. Now, as we move into a new era where the highest ideals and practices of East and West are flowing together into a greater whole, I believe that the time has come to share these teachings with a wider audience. My intention, and my heart's deepest desire, is to bring the healing influence of Living Meditation to people and families everywhere so that we can all enjoy increased wellbeing and greater connection as part of our daily lives.

Before we begin to explore the eight keys of Living Meditation, let me share one of my father's stories with you.

My father was in his orchard late one afternoon, pruning back the branches of a fruit tree, when a messenger arrived and handed him a note from his master.

In all the years he had been learning from Master Borion, he had received such a note only once before. Therefore, he opened this one with some anxiety. It said, simply, "Come quickly. I have only one day to live."

These words filled my father with unspeakable panic. He dropped his tools on the ground and ran at top speed up the pathway leading to Master Borion's cottage. When he finally arrived, breathless and drenched with perspiration, the sun was just beginning to set. A dull red glow coloured the door of the cottage. My father knocked and shouted, "Master, are you there?"

"Come in," called a voice.

With ultimate reverence, my father slowly opened the door and peered into the darkness. When his eyes grew accustomed to the faint light of a single candle burning there, he could make out the figure of his master lying on his bed. "Come closer," said the voice.

Panic now replaced with sadness, my father walked softly over to the bed, bowed in respect and choked back a sigh.

"I have something to say to you before the day ends," said Master Borion.

My father straightened up. "I am ready, Master," he said quietly.

Master Borion motioned for him to sit down and then took his hand into his own. "We come into this world with nothing. We live here for a while on borrowed goods. Then we leave with nothing."

"Borrowed goods?" said my father.

"Things of this world can make our life more comfortable," replied Master Borion. "But we must leave all such things behind when we go. All visible things are only borrowed. Where did you come from?"

"From the orchard, in response to your note."

"Before that?"

"You know my family has always lived here, ever since I was born," said my father.

"Before that?" persisted Master Borion.

My father was silent, but he knew in his heart what his master was thinking.

"Let me tell you a story," said Master Borion. "I once found a man sitting alone beneath the branches of an oak tree by the side of the road. 'Where are you coming from, and where are you going?' I asked him. 'I don't know,' he replied. 'I have forgotten.' And in truth, this man had lost all memory of who he was and what he was about."

"Whatever became of him?" my father asked, yet he was still thinking about the words "Only one day to live".

"I tended him for many seasons," replied Master Borion, "until, little by little, his light returned to him, and he remembered a home far away on a distant mountain from where he had come."

"Did he return home?" asked my father.

Master Borion smiled and clutched my father's hand a little more tightly. "As quickly as you remember where you have come from, just as quickly you know also the way to return. All life is an 'unforgetting'. That is the principle of enlightenment." Then my father, understanding that his master had been speaking about him, started to talk.

Master Borion raised his hand to invite silence. "When you are born, that is the morning. You are fresh and new as you come into this life. Life challenges you to choose good or bad. You pass through the day of your life engaged in choosing the one way or the other. Where you came from fades quickly from your mind in the cycles of life – the comings and goings, the ups and downs, the ins and outs. And when the sun begins to set, you look at your day on earth and see what fruit has come of it. Is it the noble and good seed you leave behind, or is it rotten fruit, good for nothing but to be returned to the earth and recycled for another day? What will tomorrow be like for you?"

My father swallowed, thinking that he soon would know what life would be like without the presence of his master. "Am I ready, Master?" he asked.

"When I was very young, I learned from my master in those mountains," Master Borion reminisced as he gazed through

the window toward the silhouettes of the dark peaks on the horizon. "I am still there."

"What do you mean?" asked my father.

"When you travel the Chung Doe *(mindful) pathway," replied Master Borion, "your presence endures forever. My master is there too, and his before him. The good seed lives on in the student. When I am gone, the people will see me in you. If they do not see you, they do not see me. Therefore, how urgent it is to cultivate the good seed to leave behind – harmony, balance, character, peace, empathy, happiness. That is the principle of true success in life. I will soon sleep now."*

"But, Master," objected my father, "the day is not yet over."

"Life is one day," answered Master Borion. "We have time to say, 'Good morning,' 'Good day,' 'Good night.' Can the people not for one single day seek the invisible fruit on the Chung Doe *pathway? Can they not pass the test and be ready to leave behind the good seed for their families and the coming generations?"*

"Master, what advice will you leave me, this last time?" asked my father.

Master Borion tightened his grip on my father's hand. "No matter who the people are," he said, "they have a time to be born, a time to live and a time to die. It is now my time to die. I have done the best I knew how to stay on the Chung Doe *path."*

As he listened, hanging on every word, my father felt tears welling up in his eyes. A draft of air caused the flame of the nearly spent candle to dance, as if dodging the unexpected attack.

"Chung Doe *(mindfulness, positivity) is like the candle," continued Master Borion. "It is attacked constantly by outside forces. These are* Pa Doe *(the careless and unaware path or person)."*

"And if the candle is blown out?" asked my father.

The Grand Master raised his eyebrows. "If the light goes out too soon, then, in the dark, you fail. But your candle will burn long enough. The Chung Doe *pathway leads forever upward. The higher it rises on the mountain, the greater is the force of the wind, attacking in resistance. Deep within the mountain it is quieter. That is enduring knowledge."*

My father listened in reverent silence.

"I hear the universe calling me," said Master Borion. "Time to go ... I am ready to connect with God (the universe)."

Feeling my father's sorrow, he added, "There will be a time for sadness, but not now. This is the time to use knowledge with wisdom to help others in pain who look to your light. They have more pain than you can begin to imagine. All the knowledge I have, I have given to you. There is no more. Use it with wisdom. You are the bright sun who will help so many others. When they look to you, they look to me and to all those who have come before along this path. If you fail, I fail."

"Master, I will not fail you," asserted my father.

"No!" said Master Borion firmly. "Not for me *– for* you. *Succeed for* yourself. *When you leave behind the good seeds of harmony, peace and happiness, the way is opened for others to follow in your footsteps. We are all connected. When the recognition passes to you, it passes through you to me. When you earn (fulfil your purpose), I earn. That is the*

infinite circle. It is a principle of life. This is Chung Doe. *What do you see?"*

"You have taught me well, Master, but I still have much to learn," replied my father. "How can I . . .?"

Master Borion placed the fingers of his other hand against the lips of his student. "Do as I have done, and even better. I have gone as far as I am able. You go beyond. Go further. Be a living vessel of wisdom. Take my brightness and be even brighter. Take this knowledge and go even further. When you make things better, it is better for me, too. Remember, on the Chung Doe *pathway you are never alone. I will always be there."*

"I will never forget you, Master," said my father. "You are like a father to me."

A few silent moments passed. The last glow of sunset faded into darkness.

My father spoke softly: "The darkness, it is heavy."

"And the light," replied Master Borion, "it will lift you up above the darkness to a place where your burdens will seem light as a feather. That is great spiritual strength." Master Borion tightened his grip on my father's hand, saying, "You will live your life so that you can connect with God (the universe), your first parent, and not turn your head in shame. I know you. I see you with the invisible eye. No matter what influence may come into your life, you know Chung Doe. *You know the correct way. You are your own guard. You will keep yourself always on the* Chung Doe *pathway. Because so many others are influenced by* Pa Doe *(carelessness or negativity), you will be a role model to bring them back. That is what you can do for them."*

"Is there nothing I can do for you, Master?" asked my father.

"Do this for me," he replied. "Teach others that no one escapes accountability. All must connect with God. Turn your face always toward God and travel the path of Chung Doe. *Let your light always shine for others. That is all I ask."*

The small candle flickered and went out. Relaxing his grip, Master Borion whispered, "I am tired. Now I sleep."

In that moment, something wonderful happened. Something grand passed from teacher to student. Was it the call to illuminate the pathway with the enduring light of wisdom? Was it the commission to be a bringer of peace in a world of confusion? Was it the challenge to rise even higher than this grand, sage man? Was it the spirit of harmony, togetherness, peace and joy? Was it the good seed of honour, the good name of loyalty and genuine relationships? Was it the strength to teach many families how to reach their highest potential?

In the light of all these things there sprouted in that moment a blade of new growth within my father – a new commitment, a new promise, a new covenant to share widely the knowledge he had gained, to truly earn the wisdom he had been cultivating, by giving to others. That was the quest. That was the mission: to open up to the world a better way, a purer way, a way leading to the highest form of humanness.

My father grasped the hand of Master Borion one last time. Then he gently withdrew his hand, bowed his head, and whispered to himself, "I have only one day to live." Quietly he left the cottage and started down the pathway toward home, Master Borion walking in his footsteps.

KEY ONE: KNOW YOUR TRUE SELF

In this life it is so vital to know your true self – or to say it another way: to be aware of yourself. All the answers in this life are found in nature and the universe around you, which means that all the answers can be found within yourself, because you are a microcosm of the universe.

In order to be connected to the universe and to those around us, we first have to be aware of, and present within, ourselves. Only then are we able to see ourselves, and everything around us, clearly.

It is so important to remember that you have the power to choose in everything that you do. When imbalanced situations arise that can cause stress and be overwhelming – whether it is an argument with a loved one, or tension at work or within our community – it is vital to take a moment to remember that you have the choice to react or respond to the situation that you find yourself in.

When you react, you act according to emotion, which often leads to blaming other people or the situation around you. This takes the difficulty outside of yourself, and matters can soon become chaotic and completely out of your control. When you take a moment to be aware of your own self, you are able to ground yourself and see yourself more clearly. By seeing yourself more clearly, you are in turn able to see the situation around you more clearly. Then you are able to balance with your given situation and respond, instead of reacting based on emotion.

Sometimes it's our own mind that we can't seem to control or calm. It takes awareness to realize that we are even struggling with this, but when you do become aware of it, in that moment you have the power to calm your mind and be present in the moment. By doing this you will gain so much inner strength and power. This is how we can achieve peace in our daily life no matter what is happening in our surroundings.

This is something that no one can take away from you.

This is the power of knowing your true self.

"Remember that you have the power to choose in everything that you do."

On a still, beautiful day, my father and his teacher, Master Borion, were strolling beside a crystal-clear pond. The scent of cherry blossoms filled the air.

"See the dragonfly over there, next to the lotus flower?" said Master Borion.

My father looked up at his teacher and stated, "It's sitting directly upon its own image on the water."

"What question does it ask you?" Master Borion replied.

"What do you mean?"

"It asks, 'How long have you known yourself?'" answered Master Borion.

"How long have I known myself? Well, my whole life!" said my father. "What sort of question is that?"

"How do you look?" asked Master Borion.

"The same way I look in the water. You can see my image, reflected right there," said my father, pointing.

"Close your eyes. Now, how do you look?"

Somewhat reluctantly, my father closed his eyes. "I see some of my features in my mind, but they are not clear."

"Through Living Meditation you will learn to see yourself clearly – not only the visible you, but the invisible you."

"How can I see the invisible me?"

Master Borion smiled. "The correct path begins when you humbly ask: 'Who am I?' The most important thing is to learn to know your true, pure self. That is the first step of Living Meditation. Most people, when they close their eyes, see nothing. They are gone, because their self-image is a fleeting shadow. They do not know themselves and, worse yet, they do not know that they do not know themselves."

"How can I know myself clearly?" asked my father.

"It is both a choice and a way."

"I'm confused … What do you mean?"

"It is a choice because you have the power to become as great as you want. It is a way because you can move forward day by day along the correct path toward knowing your inner self."

"Who can guide me on this path?" asked my father.

"You will guide yourself using correct principles. You are your own guide. You are your own guard, no matter where you are."

"My own guard?"

"Living Meditation is the path leading to true mental, physical and spiritual harmony. It is both dangerous and secure. For those who do not know themselves, it is a path of danger, because that which we cannot see can harm us and the

'unknowing' can damage others. That is the wrong path, the path of carelessness. But for those who see and know, Living Meditation points to a way of security, because they are their own guards. They are a light to themselves and a beacon to others. They are on the correct path – the path of mindfulness – and that is the pathway of wisdom."

"Am I on such a path?" asked my father.

"Look at what you did today. What do you see?"

"I see myself strolling and learning."

"When you learn to know your true self, your pure self," said Master Borion, "you will see yourself without using a mirror." Master Borion stopped walking for a moment. He faced my father and placed his hands on his shoulders. "Look at the spot of dirt on your face."

My father blinked his eyes in surprise. "What dirt?"

With the back of his fingers, Master Borion brushed away a spot of dirt from my father's cheek. "You could not see it nor feel it, but soon you will know with certainty when such an intrusion is present, because you will see it and feel it with your inner self. You are your own guard. If you are deep and still, you can purify yourself and be wholly aware of yourself, both visibly and invisibly."

"Deep and still?"

"Like this deep pond," replied Master Borion. "Shallow water can be noisy, with much splashing. The wrong and careless path is shallow and noisy. The correct and mindful path brings you into deep, still water that moves slowly with the way of the universe – the Tao. Depth brings forth power.

The deeper the water, the stronger the power."

"How soon will I find myself?" asked my father.

Master Borion reached down and gathered a handful of sand. "The steps you follow along the correct path are like these small grains of sand. When they are cemented together and formed into bricks, they become the building blocks of self-knowledge. I will teach you the principles, but you must act for yourself. I will bring you to the banquet of learning, but you must eat on your own and at your own pace. This is the principle of all learning."

"Is the way hard?"

"To construct the building of self-knowledge is hard, yes, but the rewards are great. Once you have finished the task, you will feel secure within your building, your temple of wisdom. You will feel at peace no matter what storms may descend upon you. Then, regardless of where you are, you will have harmony and inner peace, because the building of wisdom is within you. And with care, the building will last forever."

My father lowered his head, thinking deeply. Then, lifting his gaze to his teacher once again, he said, "How soon can I be like you? Is it even possible?"

Master Borion smiled as he caught a glimpse of the dragonfly perching on the surface of the water nearby. Concentric circles expanded in the sunlight. "It is indeed possible," said the Master. "You are now ready. Tomorrow we begin."

The Tao and Two Paths

Tao means universal truth, or you might say universal connectedness. I love that word *connectedness*. It's like plugging into the energy that is in everything: your life, your career, your relationships, as well as the natural world around you. It can be as simple as connecting to nature: that lift of your heart you experience when you look out at the ocean or walk through a forest.

When you're connected in this way, you're never alone. It also helps you detach from getting too involved emotionally in the day to day, which can be exhausting. The Tao lifts you out and yet it connects you at the same time.

The Tao has existed since the beginning of time, and in some measure it is mysterious and unexplainable. It is an anchor for me, and for many others. From the Tao comes the symbol of yin and yang, the swirling black and white circle. The yin, the dark swirl, is associated with night, femininity and quietness; the yang, the light swirl, represents brightness, daylight, masculinity and loudness. Together, yin and yang embody the dichotomy of everything in life and represent it in a beautiful way.

Throughout history the great teachers of East Asia have taught about two paths we can follow. One is the path of mindfulness, or the correct and good path, which is translated in Korean as *Chung Doe*. The other is the path of carelessness, or the blind, negative or wrong path, which is translated in Korean as *Pa Doe*.

What, we may ask, is "good"? Most ethicists and philosophers would broadly agree that the concept of good is represented by the conduct that should be preferred when we are presented with a choice between possible actions. Taoist ethics are concerned less with being good than becoming a good person who lives in harmony with all things and people, and whose actions follow through. If a Taoist wants to live well, they should take all their decisions in the context of the Tao, trying to see what will fit best and balance with the natural order of things. It is about ***being*** and ***action*** rather than ***trying***.

Right now, my son Jackson is obsessed with being a "good" boy. As I write this he is not yet three, but even so he already knows that goodness means a lot to his parents. Here's how we have explained it to him. Being a good boy means being kind, it means being thoughtful and it means acting accordingly. It means listening to your parents and your elders, having respect for others, putting yourself in others' shoes.

It is not my intention to talk about good and bad like a judgment. It's not really up to me or to any of us to decide these things. In the Tao, good is distilled as those characteristics of kindness and compassion that represent living in harmony with others.

The first step of Living Meditation is to learn to know your true (pure) self in all aspects: mental, physical, spiritual and in relationships with others. When you achieve this understanding of yourself, which is a constant and never-ending practice, you are prepared to choose and follow the correct path.

Mindfulness is one of the main principles of Living Meditation. When we develop a deep sense of self-knowledge as we follow the correct path, we will more easily remain on course.

Why is this so important? Those who follow the correct and mindful path value the principles of honour, integrity, loyalty and compassion above all else, and live their lives accordingly. Someone who follows the mindful path considers the consequences to others involved before making any decision fully. When we follow the mindful path, we build character, confidence, self-esteem and strength, which directly leads to a life of purpose and happiness.

On the other hand, when we choose to follow the wrong path, we are overtaken by egotism and jealousy, and we lack qualities such as honour, discipline and stability. We do not know ourselves and our own potential; worse still, we often do not *know* that we do not know ourselves – we are blind to or ignorant of the pure truth, and we act in a state of unknowing and disharmony. Our self-love makes us blind to the light of goodness and service to others. We are "drunk" with our small thoughts, brought down by our petty self-interests and insecurities.

Choosing Your Path

The beautiful thing is that each of us truly does have the power to choose the path that we will take. How can we choose? Firstly, by learning to know our true (pure) selves. This isn't just an isolated, egoistic exercise. It has much to do with connectedness and therefore relationships. Knowing your true self is a process that begins internally, but it is important not to *dwell* on yourself for too long. Instead, check in with yourself and see where you are standing. For example, perhaps you have lingering thoughts or emotions that you can detach from by "zooming out", then quickly moving on and applying this wisdom in your relationships and the circumstances that you are facing.

I was raised this way and I raise my children this way as well, because every decision we make is not just for this moment in time. When we decide to go down this correct path, we make sure that we continue all the good things that came before us and all of the things we wish to leave for our grandchildren's grandchildren. It's a wavelength of connectedness among people, among nature, among the time before and the time to come. This kind of "longitudinal connection" between generations and through time is one of the important tenets of Taoism and I have found that it gives me a great deal of joy as well as a sense of rootedness.

With the invisible eye, you view yourself perpetually in the image of your highest potential. The Korean term is *In Gun*, which means the highest form of humanness. No matter what your circumstances, no matter what others might say of you, no matter how you might be judged or misjudged, you are that true self that you see with the invisible eye. You are the mountain, not a fleeting wisp of smoke; the rock, not a dry leaf spiralling down in the wind; the ocean, not a dying ember in the night. You are your own true self forever, moving constantly upward along the correct pathway, toward a clear vision of absolute humanness. That is the principle of the true (pure) self. In the end, it is always your choice.

Standing Firm

Often those who travel the blind and careless path choose to fall and, when they do, they want others to fall with them. In their envy, jealousy and insecurity, they seek to disrupt the path of the mindful. They may say, "The mountain is going to cave in. The rock is going to crumble. The ocean is mere vapour." To those who are uncertain, this verbal weapon is terrifying. But to the self-knowing person this weapon is no weapon at all, because the self-knowing person is anchored in the vision of who they truly are.

What this tells me is that regardless of how someone treats me, I can choose to respond with kindness, compassion and openness. Above all I can put myself in their shoes. When I was about nineteen years old, I was getting a table in a restaurant for my father, mother and me. The hostess gave me some attitude; she was being irritable and totally unhelpful. I was just about to react to her when my father took my arm and looked at me. I was pretty sure I knew what he was going to say – after all, I was nineteen, so I knew everything!

"Why is she treating me that way? What is her problem?"

"Munchkin," my father said (that's what he called me, even when I was a grown woman!) "How do you know what she has walked through? Number one, how do you know what has happened to her this morning? And number two, why do you even let that bother you?"

In that moment and in many others since then, I had to continue to choose the correct path, no matter what others were doing around me – and maybe particularly if they were hostile to me, because I could never know what had brought them to choose that path.

We simply can't listen to and absorb everything that people say. Ultimately, we have the choice to respond in a manner that balances the situation, or react, which usually gives way to tension and arguments. Whether it's on social media, in schoolyard chatter or water-cooler banter, we can take just one moment to pause and think rather than jumping on the bandwagon of gossiping about others or trying to knock people down. Just imagine the difference it would make if we all lived as a community where we felt truly connected as human beings.

This idea is nothing new, of course. Throughout history, people of character have learned how to stand firm even in the face of gossip and rumours. In Living Meditation, the mindful person deflects negativity in three key ways:

1. Grounding yourself – and staying focused on your true (pure) self. Look at yourself with your invisible eye.

2. Gaining perspective – and gathering the facts. When gossip begins, practise and encourage others in the principle of not drawing any conclusions in the absence of observable, confirmed facts. Bring light into the situation before making any judgments or acting on information supplied by others.

3. Taking action – and continuing to move forward and upward on the correct path, no matter what. Refuse to be distracted and, if you find that you have been, acknowledge it and get back on track. Life constantly challenges us to choose good or bad. This you cannot change, but you can continually endeavour to choose the good way.

There is a higher path that needs to be pursued: marriages that need to be purified so that no negative elements can come in; children who need to be given direction and shown how to live by principle; communities that need to be given more enlightened leadership. All of this depends on knowing the true self.

In the true self, there is great power to ward off the hurtful forces swirling all around us that would dim the light of self-knowledge and override our principles. These forces wither in the face of mindfulness like blades of grass in a blazing furnace.

How to Cultivate a Relationship without Cracks

Learning to know our true and pure self means knowing ourselves in four aspects: physically, mentally, spiritually and in relationship with others. To gain genuine balance and harmony, the mindful person trains their mind, body and spirit to draw from the limitless reserve of energy in the universe. They align their actions with natural and eternal principles, so they can be aware of and purge negative influences before they have a destructive effect.

The same applies to the mindful way of building relationships. Good relationships endure because they are rooted in the principle of mutual understanding and respect, as well as the goal of cultivating a lasting legacy for our family as a whole and the coming generations. Purity of relationship is an essential part of Living Meditation. Just as we guard against exposing our body to germs and viruses, we should also guard against allowing damaging influences to enter our relationships. If there is even a tiny crack in the relationship, toxic elements can creep in.

Pure friendship and pure love characterize the relationship between and among those who are mindful. Their relationships remain open to new ideas, creative solutions and loving suggestions, and there is a commitment to striving to "lift" one another. The greatest relationships are those where each person works to help the other become that much better. At the same time, these relationships resist antagonism, envy and any influence that produces disrespect, lack of connection, jealousy or the destruction of another person.

In marriage, in friendships and in business, relationships often erode because people become misaligned and harmony fades. People who endeavour to strengthen a relationship through sheer willpower and heroic effort often fail. A metal rod bent and straightened repeatedly over and over again at the same spot will become brittle and eventually snap. The same thing can happen in a relationship.

From the moment that my husband Craig and I were in a relationship, we thought about this. We shared the visual image of a foundation without any cracks. My father always raised me to see the individuals in our family like two hands making a clap. What he meant was this: when you are family, it is important to ask yourself, *What am I trying to achieve? What is my point in trying to argue? What good truly comes from one family member "winning" over the other?* Your intention should be to go one step deeper to that foundation and make sure there are no cracks. Understand the purpose and intention of where that other person is coming from too, because almost always you want to end up in the same place. For Craig and me, it's very important in our relationship, because not only are we married, we also work together and we have children together. For every situation you're in, you can constantly reflect upon yourself and your relationships. This is a true demonstration of Living Meditation.

Picture the scene: Let's say you walk into a disordered room in your house. Toys and plates and cups are strewn everywhere, the windows are smeared with grime, and there is dirt on every surface. You know you have to clean it up. Now, consider: how often you look inside yourself in the same way?

My belief is that one of the things you can do to make sure that you remain a mindful person is to realize that *there's always purification that needs to happen*. I like to think of it as a spiritual and emotional form of Marie Kondo's philosophy of the life-changing magic of tidying up. A couple of years ago I wrote a blog post, "It's time to clean up on the inside", and I chose to illustrate it with a picture of a big wheelbarrow full of garbage. I wanted people to see and understand that just as we can tidy our homes, we can also tidy up on the inside. And, as we all know, you don't just tidy up the once; it's an ongoing job. Ideally, we should always be looking out for clutter and removing it before it builds up. If you think of it that way, Living Meditation is like the KonMari Method for decluttering your house, but applied to your inner self!

This is the work we need to do to reveal our true selves. It is necessary for each individual to learn their true self and cultivate good relationships that reflect the values of balance, integrity, loyalty, trust and commitment. Enduring relationships are sustained by such wisdom and practice.

One thing to understand about pure love is that it is not closed in. When we are in a pure relationship, we are never too close, yet never too far away from each other. We stand in just the right proximity. If we pull too close, the relationship can become brittle and break. If it is maintained too loosely, or becomes disconnected, other influences can wedge themselves in between us and start their work of destruction. But if the relationship is flexible, balanced and rooted in common goals, then both people will act as their true selves and work toward achieving and maintaining harmony, balance, happiness and growth, transforming the bond into one that endures forever.

Stronger Than Truth

You may think there is nothing stronger than a relationship founded on truth. I want to challenge your thinking on that. A promise written in the sand, a nest built in tumbleweed – all of these are more enduring than a relationship built on momentary truth.

In all relationships, there comes a time when people open up to each other to bare their innermost thoughts and feelings. This is the "moment of truth". They say to themselves, "We have revealed our deepest souls to each other. Now we have lasting trust between us, because we know things about each other that no one else knows."

But this momentary truth is not a solid foundation for a relationship. Such truth can change, because it comes from thoughts. Thoughts come from the mind, and is the mind not always changing? How can a relationship be safely anchored to a drifting dock? When that truth changes in one person, the other is often unaware of the transition to a new momentary truth. Discovering it after the fact is often a shock. It results in hurt and anger, and then the relationship erodes from one that is close and harmonious to one that is distant and troubled.

It doesn't need to be this way. A relationship built on principle endures, because principle never changes. Principle is eternal truth, a solid anchor for a relationship. A solid foundation.

If you learn to see yourself with the invisible eye, you are filled with confident hope for the future and certainty about success. You know your identity: you are not smoke or a dry leaf or a dying ember, but a mountain, a rock, an ocean. This certainty imparts strength to your relationships, your spouse and your children. It makes your bonds last forever.

Be Deep Like the Ocean

In the story earlier in this chapter, Master Borion explains the difference between deep water and still water.

Pa Doe, the wrong and careless path, is shallow and noisy. *Chung Doe*, the correct and mindful path, brings you into deep, still water that moves slowly with the way of the universe. Depth brings forth power. The deeper the water, the stronger the power.

More than anything, my ultimate wish is to be deep like the ocean, feeling the current of the universe but not being tossed around by every wind that hits me. Living like that is exhausting. With so much chaos happening inside ourselves, life flies by, we get stressed and we become unwell – physically, mentally and spiritually. We cannot be good partners, good daughters, good sons, good friends, good parents. It's a domino effect.

There's a saying:

Watch your thoughts, they become words;
watch your words, they become actions;
watch your actions, they become habits;
watch your habits, they become character;
watch your character for it becomes your destiny.

You have to be aware of your thoughts and your words and then know that those thoughts and those words reflect exactly how you will act in this life. They will all align, for better or worse.

Here is another way of thinking about deep water versus shallow. Every kind of water has its own sound and the true self has an ear that discerns the difference. Likewise, our true self listens to the voices of those who are on the path of mindfulness and chooses relationships correctly and wisely. There are three main kinds of voices in this world:

1. The voice of mindfulness: Words, tones and volume that cultivate harmony, balance, togetherness, respect, awareness and dignity. The intention is compassion and cultivating good seeds for the future. The communication is direct, clear, dignified, humble – like deep, still water that moves unstoppably forward with power and purpose.

2. The voice of superficiality: Words, tones and volume that only serve to fill the silence with small talk and aimless superficialities. The intention is to spend time and gain attention. The communication is rambling, circular, shallow – like the eddies going nowhere at the edge of a stream.

3. The voice of ignorance: Words, tones and volume designed to secure specific personal benefit or advantage to the speaker. The nature of such a voice is self-serving. The intention is often manipulation. The tone is shrill, boastful and arrogant. The volume is loud, like the frantic, muddy downpour of wash in the gutter after a sudden storm: quick, boisterous and shadowed with negativity.

When we are on the correct path, we have the ability to discern these different voices and choose to align ourselves only with those of awareness, connectedness and mindfulness.

No One Can Eat for You

Each time you read the Tao, it can mean something different to you. It is a little enigmatic, a little elusive, and that can be uncomfortable for us. In the Western mentality, we want answers. We want specifics. We want the solution, and we want it right now. And yet, much of the time, that's not how life works. Usually, you need to walk the path. No one else can feed you the answers – or, as my father would say to me, "No one can eat for you."

I hope that this book has a little of that quality: it offers the principles you need, but *you* have to eat the food; *you* have to make it your own.

This is how I was raised. My father never took the quick solution. Instead, he would challenge me to consider my own behaviour.

Sometimes that was frustrating for me. "Daddy, why don't you just ground me like all the other parents do?" But no, he would sit me down and take the time to explain things to me, plant seeds in my mind. He was both my parent and my teacher, and he would always take the time to illuminate these principles for me and then help me apply them to my reality: if you go down this road, there's a very good chance this is going to happen. It was a very logical approach. If you're an intelligent human being, you cannot argue with it.

Now, with my own children, when they're doing something that is unwise, I try to take the time to stop and walk them through it.

"Jackson, if you keep playing with the car window button, what's going to happen?"

"I'm going to squish my finger."

"And is that going to feel good?"

"No…"

"Okay. So do you want to keep playing with the window?"

"No, Mommy."

As a child, I was the kind of girl who didn't like to ruffle too many feathers. But I would sometimes get in trouble for something that my father would call "looking for attention". At age seven, I didn't really even know what that was. My father would say, "Munchkin, stop looking for attention." Boy, did that hit me in a different way when I became a parent. I find myself saying that to my oldest son now. It's the times when a child acts up in a surprising way, or goes and pouts in the corner instead of going to Mommy or Daddy and asking directly for something they want.

Even adults can have a difficult time being straight and authentic! It's that voice of superficiality I described earlier. Children often need help communicating their thoughts, feelings and wants, and it is important to help them decode these things, such as the feeling of being left out or why something might be making them angry. They may lack the awareness that what they are doing is a signal that they need something specific from parents, or they may simply lack the language skills needed to verbalize that what they need is compassion or conscious attention, or simply peace, food or sleep! But without these patterns being decoded for us, we carry the same behaviours into adulthood – for example, sulking when we actually want to talk. Silence when we need a hug. Being able to tune into what you *actually* need and are asking for is a skill that will give you wind in your sails through life's inevitable choppy waters.

This sounds like such a little thing, but these principles bring a sense of confidence, security and peace. When you start to know yourself well enough, you don't have to look for attention elsewhere. So long as you are on this mindful path of compassion and kindness and having good intention, you can be solid in the ways you go about living your life.

This Is Your First Step

Learning to know your true self is the beginning of your journey along the upward-rising mindful path. The journey is not without its obstacles, for life never ceases to challenge us to choose good or bad.

The path never stops – for any of us. I know that I am not *there*, and I don't know if I ever will be. There is always more to learn, but the beautiful part is that these thoughts and these practices eventually become habitual, so we don't have to think about it so much anymore. It becomes part of our daily living. That's what Living Meditation looks like.

By choosing the mindful way, you will come to know your great mental, physical and spiritual capacity and grow to fulfil this limitless potential. You will build pure relationships that will help you cultivate good seeds to leave for your family and others for generations to come: the good seeds of harmony, balance, peace, joy, loyalty and lasting togetherness.

KEY TWO: THE TRUE-RIGHT-CORRECT METHOD

In my eyes, one of the ultimate goals in this life is to reach a certain kind of awakening or enlightenment, to be able to see more clearly and to know myself well. This to me is a very East Asian perspective. Many people find that awakening through meditation and considering the life of Buddha – whether they are Buddhist or not. There's also an understanding, particularly in East Asian culture, that awakening can be reached through calligraphy or the movements of Tai Chi. Awakening can even be reached through music. If you put your mind and your heart fully into something, even something as simple as making food, there is enlightenment to be had.

Enlightenment is present in the way you look at everything. And by taking that stance, you are always present – or perhaps always moving *toward* being present, because it's a constant practice.

When you look at life this way, every moment is precious.

In the first key of Living Meditation, we have seen the importance of choosing a path. This choice is not a "one and done" thing. Every day we are faced with another set of fresh choices to make. What to do when our child wants our help with a school project? How to respond when a colleague makes a serious mistake at work? When we see a stranger in trouble, should we jump in or stand back?

You might say that having chosen a path, we now need a method to navigate it – and that is exactly what this second key offers us.

After nature had poured a gentle rain over the earth, the dawn brought warmth to the countryside. Footsteps announced a visitor to Master Borion's cottage. It was my father, who gingerly knocked on the door. "Master, are you awake?"

"Over here," called a voice from behind an apple tree in a neighbouring orchard. Startled, my father turned and peered into the rising sun in the direction of the voice.

"Is that you, Master?"

"Yes."

"I am sorry to be a little late," my father called, "but the pillow held me prisoner."

"You wanted to stay in bed this morning?"

"No! That is, I ..." stammered my father.

"Speak the truth!"

"Well, it was inviting."

"Why didn't you follow your true feelings and stay in bed?" asked Master Borion.

"Because I had an appointment to see you and receive a lesson. It was right to come."

"Your lesson has already started," replied Master Borion. "You did the right thing to come. Those three friends – the true, the right and the correct – they are your companions for life. Go to the deepest valley and they are there. Go to the highest mountain and they are there. Cross the widest sea and they are already waiting for you. How you deal with these three companions will determine your course in life and how much peace you will enjoy."

"Can you explain a little more, Master?"

Master Borion smiled. "Here, let's pick some fruit. How do you feel about these apples? Don't they look delicious? Go ahead. Pick one."

"Well, they look good, and I came away in a hurry without any breakfast."

"So you truly want one?" asked Master Borion.

"Well, yes, that's true, but ..."

"What if I told you that the farmer gave me permission to take fruit from this tree?" asked Master Borion, as he reached up and picked one of the most beautiful apples.

"Then it would be the correct thing to do ...?" replied my father a little hesitantly.

Master Borion handed him the apple. "Already you are beginning to understand. Hold on to this apple until we get to the village. I have someone I want you to meet."

As the two made their way down the puddled roadway, a woman on a loaded bicycle dashed past them. Her bicycle tire hit a pothole full of rainwater and sent a spray of mud over my father.

"Hey!" he shouted angrily. "Look what you've done to me!"

Embarrassed, the woman stopped and returned to her victim. "I am so sorry," she said, "I didn't want to be late opening up my stall at the market."

"What do you sell?" asked Master Borion, as my father dabbed at the mud on his sleeve.

"I weave baskets at night and sell them during the day to feed my family."

"What time do you have to get up each morning?"

"Four o'clock."

"Do you like getting up so early?" he asked.

"No," she replied. "But I must work to care for my family. That is the right thing for me to do."

"Is it right for you to leave your children all day?" Master Borion teased gently.

"Honestly, I would rather care for them myself," replied the woman, "and it's not right to leave them. But I must work to give them food."

"You act correctly," Master Borion assured her. "Your children will benefit from this correct judgment. And for this you will

have peace. I'm sure you have left your children in good hands. Have a pleasant day."

After the woman had pedalled away, Master Borion looked at my father and asked, "Do you always conduct your life according to that which is true?"

"Of course," replied my father, somewhat offended at the question.

"How did you feel when that woman splashed you with mud?"

"I felt like pushing her off the roadway and into the ditch," replied my father peevishly.

"That was your true feeling?"

"Yes."

"Then, if you always act according to that which is true, why didn't you do it?"

"Well," mumbled my father, "I guess I decided it would not be the right thing to do."

"By controlling your actions in this way," replied Master Borion, "you did that which was correct. You are a good host to your three companions – the true, the right and the correct. The way of the Living Meditation path is to balance the true with the right and arrive at the correct."

By now Master Borion and my father had reached the village, where the marketplace was buzzing with noise and activity.

"Follow me," said Master Borion. The two made their way down a dark alley to a dingy shack in an isolated corner of the village.

"Look through this window and tell me what you see," directed Master Borion.

My father shielded his eyes from the morning sun and peered into the darkness. He saw inside the shack an old man in rags, cowering in the corner.

"A homeless man," said my father. "How does he put up with the cold and the misery of this place?"

"Hello, my friend," said Master Borion to the stranger. "How do you feel today?"

"I endure," whispered the man. "Thank you for coming again."

Turning to my father, Master Borion enquired, "How do you feel about this old man suffering alone here?"

"I would truly like to rescue him from his misery."

"Then why don't you do it? You can find a way to change things for him."

"I see that it wouldn't be right," said my father, "for how can any single action of mine rescue him?"

"Then you will do nothing?"

My father hesitated for a minute, not knowing what to do. Then suddenly he smiled broadly. "I will give him this apple. It's a start."

"That is correct," said Master Borion. "Though you would truly like to rescue him, it isn't in your hands to do so. So, in this moment, it is correct not to do so. Although you would truly like to eat the apple yourself – and it would normally be right to do so – in this case it is right to care for this stranger. You may do the correct thing now."

Beaming with joy, my father reached through the window and handed the apple to the homeless man.

"Bless you, young man," he said. "And bless your teacher, for he has taught you kindness in your youth."

As Master Borion and my father returned to the countryside, they felt the rays of the sun warming their bodies.

"How do you feel?" asked Master Borion.

"I have joy and I have peace," my father replied.

"Joy and peace are the fruits of balance," Master Borion affirmed. "And balance is reached through correct living. Just as the sun frees you from the shadow of night, choosing the correct way will free you from the shadow of selfishness, imbalance and lack of honour. That is true harmony, the path to a successful and meaningful life. Now, let's go and pick more apples."

"How can I learn more, Master?"

"In the next lesson."

The Way of True-Right-Correct

The story of Master Borion and my father exploring what is "true, right and correct" is one of many such stories passed down for centuries, from generation to generation and from one mentor to their student, to another, to the next, through an enduring oral tradition. It's rather lovely to reflect on the fact that this isn't just *one* teacher–student relationship. Rather, this is part of a long, long chain of principles based on living in harmony with the Tao. It means a lot to me to know that certain ideas have passed the test of time.

The Way of True-Right-Correct (or the True-Right-Correct Method) has also been handed down over the centuries to help us make the correct decisions for daily living. It is a method that can be used in any and every situation to gain perspective, see a circumstance clearly and respond in a balanced and effective manner. Some might also call it the "conscience".

By knowing your true self – as we learned in the first key – you will know your true feelings, what is true for you in a given situation. From that starting point, you are able to use the Way of True-Right-Correct to increase wellbeing for yourself, your family and others, and achieve great internal strength, peace and freedom.

This method is based on a formula of relationships.

The Way of True-Right-Correct

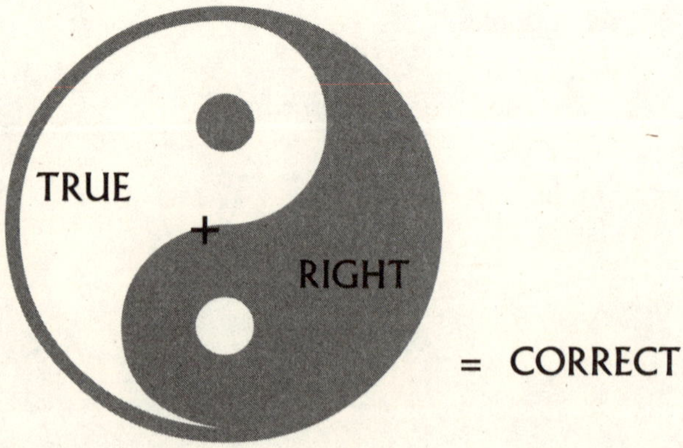

The ***true*** refers to your inner state at any given time – how you truly feel about something. This inner state might be joy, anger, fear, sadness or love. How you feel about something (the true) largely determines what you choose to do about it. In this way, the true leads to one or more possible actions in response to the circumstances at hand.

THE TRUE ⟶ ACTION COURSES

But which, if any, of these possible actions is the right thing to do under the circumstances? By ***right*** I mean what *appears* to provide the most good for everyone involved. It is often based upon what is generally accepted as a proper action, or the "black and white" of a situation.

The choice of action that will do the most good for everyone involved is called the ***correct*** choice. It is taking into account what is true to you and also taking a moment to put yourself in other people's shoes so that you can gain perspective and see the situation more clearly from all angles. Our goal is to do that which is correct in all aspects of daily living: personal, professional, spiritual; in community, work, marriage, friendship and family relationships.

The true, when balanced with the right, leads to the correct. In this way, the formula serves as a guide to help us achieve correct behaviour in daily life based on principles of balance and harmony.

TRUE + RIGHT = CORRECT

Find the Peaks and Valleys

The beauty of this symbol is that the shapes within it have meaning. The yin and yang symbol represents the consistent and ever-changing balance that exists in the Tao or the universe, in which every human being is part of a larger design.

There are constantly different ways to arrive at the ***correct*** decision: it is dynamic, active, ever-changing … and it can be challenging. However, as it becomes a habit in our daily lives, the rewards for ourselves, for our relationships and for the world around us are endless.

When I look at this symbol I reflect, too, that life is constantly flowing, with peaks and valleys – wherever there is an up, there is also a down. In life, this fact is inescapable. Yet in the midst of these ups and downs, we can find consistency, we can anchor ourselves and plug in to the flow. With our anchor, we can strive never to be too up or too down. When things are going well we can be happy and grateful, and enjoy that moment. At the same time, we know that nothing ever stays at the peak. I don't mean this in a pessimistic way, but in a realistic way! When we are down in a valley, we can remember that this is only one moment in time and there will be an up again.

It is vital to always remain grounded and consistent.

This is true balance in life.

Using the Way of True-Right-Correct to balance the true and the right and achieve the correct in daily living, allows us to reach the milestones of achievement along this journey.

How to Apply the True-Right-Correct Method in Our Daily Life?

The True-Right-Correct Method is an extraordinary tool. If we look at it with our invisible eye, we gain clarity about how it helps us make correct decisions, which are *based* on, but *transcend*, those made after considering the true or the right.

You can apply it everywhere, all the time, with your children, your spouse, in your friendships, at work or with your parents.

Suppose you notice one of your children struggling with a homework problem. Naturally you feel deep compassion for your child. So, the "true" in this case is compassion. What should be done? You think through some possibilities:

1. Scold your child for lack of self-reliance;

2. Solve the problem for your child;

3. Instruct the child to ask their teacher for help the next day;

4. Teach your child the principles behind the problem and let them follow through on their own.

Number 2 is the fastest solution and often it seems the easiest way forward in the moment. However, this is probably one of the hardest challenges as a parent: to refrain from always doing things for our children. Because if we do that, how are we helping them develop and become strong and able individuals? Right now we're talking about one homework problem, but in life, what's the balance?

I think of my father here, and how much room he gave me to make my own decisions, but he would also watch me so that I never fell off a cliff. This is such a fine line to tread – to let someone make their own decisions and encourage them to the best of your ability.

In this case, let's say you wish to cultivate self-respect and independent thinking in your child, so you choose action 4, which turns out to be the correct choice in this case. (Assuming they aren't working through high-school physics that is beyond your comprehension!) There may be circumstances where the other choices would be correct, but not in this example.

This question extends beyond your children. I feel this with my mom. I feel this with my close friends. I feel this with my husband. There are times where I want to step in and protect them from difficulties, but that's not always the best way to go about things. And I'm sure they feel the same with me. How do you express love for the people you care about the most?

Just before my father passed, all three of us kids – we're not kids anymore, of course, but in a sense we were then – were sitting at lunch with our father. We did this quite often, but usually my son Vince would be with me, or my mom. On this day, it so happened it was just the three of us and my father. As we were sitting together, he said, "You know, as your father, I see each one of you. And the most important thing to me as a father is to see each one of you, and help you to achieve everything you wish to achieve, based on *you*." This was a really beautiful moment that I think none of us will ever forget. Not only is it a beautiful thought, but he acted on it. I'm different from my sister and from my brother and they are different from me, and he really did look at each one of us. He considered the circumstances that were correct for us as individuals.

My father often spoke of seeing circumstances from a "better situation", by which he meant having a better perspective. For example, suppose you are walking down the street and see a man bolt suddenly from a store and knock another man to the ground. Your first impression is that this behaviour is violent and cruel. Your "momentary truth" is that the man from the store is the aggressor and needs to be stopped. You are strongly motivated to rescue the man on the ground. Based on your current level of understanding, this action would be right.

But wait. A woman then runs out of the store and points to the man on the ground, who is now struggling to free himself from his captor. "He stole my purse," she screams. At that point, you notice the downed man is clutching a woman's purse within the folds of his jacket. This throws new light on the situation and you immediately step in and help to restrain him.

By gaining more perspective on the situation, you are able to observe things in a wider context and in greater detail. Your mind has extended its span of understanding significantly, so that you are now seeing more clearly what was unclear for you earlier. At the same time, you are now seeing from far away (from the perspective of unchanging principle) what was earlier too close to you (your "momentary truth"). Now you are more likely to choose the correct course of action.

By using the True-Right-Correct Method, you are able to see distant things up close and close things at a distance. You begin to rise to the level of wisdom, where your actions will begin to produce the good seeds of balance, harmony, peace and joy.

I was always raised to think of the difference between knowledge and wisdom in a very Confucian way. Both are equally important in Living Meditation. Knowledge is something that we can acquire through reading the teachings of great thinkers and that we can replicate, but wisdom is something that you gain only through experience and time. Whenever I say the word *wisdom*, it means something very particular. To me, wisdom is the perfect word to describe the application of the True-Right-Correct Method.

At work, when I am with my team in our manufacturing labs, I use this method all the time. Sometimes it takes the emotion out of a situation. There's nothing wrong with emotion, but making quick decisions based on emotion can be inaccurate, even dangerous. Acting on emotion is a *reaction* rather than a response. For example, there can be times when an employee makes a minor mistake that could cost the business dearly. You can imagine some bosses responding with anger, shouting at the employee and reprimanding them. This might cause some employees to shudder internally, become insecure about their future position in the company and stifle their creativity. But by stepping back and looking at the whole picture, correct action for the entire situation can be achieved. It is *true* that the employee has made an error. Is the *right* response to reprimand them? Or is there a response that transcends what is true and right and arrives at a larger outcome – the *correct* one? With that perspective we can consider how we might prevent this mistake happening in the future: whether we need more eyes on a certain procedure or an additional step in our process and, quite possibly, empower our employee by letting them know we are in this together and that we will devise a solution together to prevent this in the future. With the True-Right-Correct Method we can see close things at a distance and arrive at a decision that brings about the most good for the most people.

Doe Chi – Being Drunk on One's Own Thoughts

When we are unable to make correct decisions, all too quickly we wander from the way that leads to a balanced decision. We make decisions based only on the true or only on the right, without thinking of the correct. This *Pa Doe* pathway (the path of unawareness) is based on selfishness, greed, boastfulness and careless use of power, and leads to negativity and dead-end detours.

When we neglect to make decisions based on the Way of True-Right-Correct, we have no true power and no true freedom. Proud people often fool themselves, believing that they have power when they do not. Arrogance deceives us into believing that we have freedom, when really we have no freedom at all. Those who follow the *Pa Doe* path are on an island all by themselves. They are ruler. They own everything on their island. But what does this mean? Because they are alone, it means nothing. When you are alone, you talk only to the wind.

When we follow the blind and careless path, we hear only what we want to hear. We then use our "selective hearing" to our advantage. We ease our own pain by thriving on the pain of others, whether we mean to or not. We relish gossip. We thrive on belittling others. We pretend to help them, when in truth we are trying to increase our own worth. Instead of arriving at a correct decision, we think and act with ego and self-promotion. We aspire to the top, but our strategy delivers us straight to the bottom.

In this day and age in particular, we can filter out the things we don't want to hear. We can block someone on Facebook when their ideas offend us, we can allow the Google algorithm to select news sources that confirm our beliefs. To some extent that is just being human, but when it starts to affect how we treat others and the decisions we make in life – even how we treat ourselves – we need to draw a line. Being permanently in a likeminded bubble may feel more comfortable, but it means you're not allowing your life to have the full balance it needs, and you can begin to lose empathy for different ways of thinking and being. Always, somewhere in the back of our minds, we can choose to put ourselves in other people's shoes before making a decision or a judgment.

Ultimately, we can become drunk on our own thoughts. In the Korean language, this is reflected in the term *Doe Chi*. Under the influence of *Doe Chi* we suffer from tunnel vision, where we can only see a narrow space directly in front of our eyes; only the things that concern our own selves, never the whole picture. How can you arrive at correct decisions for the good of everyone involved when you see only yourself, alone within your confined space?

Consider a vase. How do you judge its condition? If you look at the vase from one side only and see no cracks, you could conclude that the vase is whole. But what if there are cracks on the hidden side?

If you do not see the complete picture, you cannot arrive at correct decisions.

Three Levels of Light

The true is perceived by the same part of your brain that gathers sensations through the senses (sight, hearing, touch, taste, smell). These sensations combine to give you a first wave of perception, which registers upon your mind and contributes to how you "feel" about your experience in a given moment. What you feel in a given moment is what is true for you – the "truth of the moment".

Continuing this parallel with the senses, I want to suggest to you that the True-Right-Correct Method operates on the basis of three kinds of light:

Level One – Dim Light (perception of the senses): We have the impression that this level of light is very bright. We believe that we see things clearly in all of their colours. However, this is a delusion.

Such light is very dim. It illuminates only enough to give us momentary truth, and momentary truth, as we have seen, can change very quickly.

Many actions down through the centuries have been based on momentary truth, which often leads to misunderstanding, strained relationships, disagreement and anger. What has seemed right at the moment has produced not more harmony, but less.

For example, if you have skipped a meal or two, you feel very hungry, but as soon as you eat you are not hungry anymore. What was wholly true at one moment quickly changed in another moment.

Level Two – Moderate Light (understanding of the mind): By expanding our perspective and integrating what we perceive into the larger body of our experience over time, we bring yet more light into the situation. Our actions, therefore, are more likely to be correct.

Even this is not sufficient, however. Based only on our perceptions and understanding, our right decisions may not produce the most good for the most people and thus are not correct. What is missing is the enduring connection to the Tao – unchanging principle and the world around us.

Level Three – Bright Light (wisdom of the inner eye): When we open the inner eye (the invisible eye) and view the situation from the perspective of unchanging principle, we make our decisions based on wisdom. Such decisions are always correct, because wisdom guides us to act in the interests of producing more harmony, peace, joy, vitality and lasting strength for everyone involved.

The Way of True-Right-Correct guides us to higher and higher levels of light and wisdom. As we progress along the mindful pathway and gain more experience and wisdom, we will come to make correct decisions quite naturally using this higher form of light.

It is very much like passing by someone who is eating a delicious red apple. Your mouth waters automatically. Your sensation comes from your experience of eating apples. In the same way, when you come to use wisdom naturally, you will know very quickly what is correct in life. That is the operation of the higher light, leading to the greatest benefits that endure forever.

Living Meditation Infuses Everything

When you first start to think about using the True-Right-Correct Method, sifting through what is true, what is right and what is correct seems like a burden. But after a while you find yourself doing it naturally. This is the state of Living Meditation.

Whatever you want in life and no matter how old you are, you can reach your goals – even surpass them – by using this method to guide your decisions. Use it in governing all areas of your life, especially in your treatment of marriage, children, parents, friendship, health (physical and mental), employment, personal actions and humanity. Nothing is too great or too small to benefit from the Way of True-Right-Correct.

My father truly lived his life this way. Everything was thought through. He could think and move so fast, and be sharp without any apparent effort. But as quick as his mind could be, he also had a slow-moving aspect to him. It goes back to that concept of being deep, like the depths of the ocean versus the choppy surface.

There is one thing in particular my father taught me that I often find myself returning to with my own children. I have always multitasked a lot, always had a million things going on at once. He would watch me and say, "Munchkin, how many things are you doing?"

I'd get a lot of things done, and he appreciated that about me, but sometimes he'd say, "Finish one first."

When I felt like I had a million balls in the air, it was a reminder to me to focus my mind. It's fine to balance many tasks, considerations and priorities – and some of us have no choice but to do so – but make sure that you can put your mind into one thing and finish that one task.

Just today, I found that I had to remind myself of this – complete one thing and prioritize, instead of setting it aside for later, or else all of these "things" will start to pile up! I was walking through my house in quite a hurry when I spotted a little piece of something on the ground, a plastic wrapper that someone had dropped. How often we might walk by that and think, *I must pick that up later*. Or if we have a dirty dish, leaving it on the counter to wash it later. I was raised that if you have a dirty dish, you clean it right then and there. If you're walking somewhere and you see some garbage in your path, you pick it up and throw it away. Don't wait for someone else to do it; don't wait for later. Small things, sure, but life is made up of such small things.

Through Living Meditation, you are putting your mind into your life.

Remember: unless you stay firmly in charge of your forward progress by following your inner guide, there is no direction. Without using your head in this way, how can you feel your heart? With no heart there is no hope. With no hope, there is no life. There would be nothing. Yet with the outcomes of Living Meditation – balance, harmony, strength and peace – all things are possible.

"The Way of True-Right-Correct has been handed down over the centuries to help us make the correct decisions for daily living"

KEY THREE: STOP BEING DRUNK ON YOUR OWN THOUGHTS

When we rely solely on our current thoughts and beliefs, we see life with tunnel vision. Our perspective becomes limited and self-interest often becomes our one and only motivator. When we are too "zoomed in", we can only see a narrow space in front of us, never the whole picture. We can't see people or relationships clearly, and we don't behave in our own best interests or the best interests of those around us. It's like a form of drunkenness.

Just as you may not see clearly if you are drunk from alcohol, you can also be so "drunk" on your own thoughts that you can't see your surroundings clearly anymore. The deeper you go into this state, the more you immerse yourself in this new version of reality. As we learned in the last chapter, the Korean term for this is *Doe Chi*.

To think of it another way, it's as if we are wearing sunglasses all day and night and complaining that everything is too dark – and then getting upset and demanding that someone turn the lights on.

When we keep our sunglasses on, our perspective is restricted, and our clear vision of a person or a situation is limited as well.

In order to see life clearly, release stress, have more compassion for others and gain happiness in our day-to-day existence, it is of utmost importance to gain more perspective – to *zoom out*. Take your sunglasses off and see the world as it truly is.

On a windy spring afternoon, Master Borion and my father made their way slowly up a hillside.

"It takes a lot of strength to climb uphill against the wind," my father observed.

"It does indeed," agreed Master Borion. "Life is a challenge for good or for bad through choosing good you gain strength. Through strength you will find freedom and liberty. If there is no strength, there is no hope and no freedom. With freedom there is peace."

"What do you mean?" asked my father.

"See that great tree over there? What do you hear?"

"I hear the wind rustling in the leaves, and I hear the branches brushing together and the trunk creaking."

"Do you hear the root?" asked Master Borion.

"No, of course not."

"The root is growling like a tiger."

"Growling like a tiger?" asked my father. "I can't hear anything."

"Listen. The root roars out a lesson. If you have ears, you can

hear that which is still. If you have eyes, you can see that which is invisible."

"Help me understand, Master."

"The rustling leaves and flowers are but temporary. They do their part, then they are gone – the mere shadow of life. The branches sway and weave in the wind, bending with every gust. The trunk hardly moves, because it is stronger against outside pressures. But the real strength is in the root. The root is impervious to outside pressures. This is the visible/invisible strength."

"Visible/invisible?"

"Visible to the outer eye through the growth of the tree. And the invisible strength of the root you can see with your inner eye and feel with your heart. Without this visible/invisible strength of the root, the tree will die."

"And without the branches and leaves the tree will also die," replied my father.

His teacher smiled. "Seasons come and seasons go. From time to time the gardener wisely prunes back the branches. The autumn winds carry away the leaves. But the root endures."

"I see what you mean, Master, but my eyes are captivated by the visible movement of the beautiful blossoms and leaves."

"They too speak a lesson," replied Master Borion. "Too easily they forget their invisible connections to the root. They swirl and twirl every which way the wind dictates. They hustle and bustle freely in the air. They speak with the voice of Doe Chi. *They travel on the* Pa Doe *pathway, the path of carelessness. Their beauty is short-lived. The enduring beauty is in the root, because the root has visible/invisible strength.*

The root speaks with the voice of humanness at its root centre. Such is the voice you hear on the mindful pathway of principle and wisdom. Look again at the tree. What do you see now?"

"I see now the branches and the trunk of the tree."

"The limbs sway and return to their place," replied Master Borion. "When they sway, they depart again and again from the true straight path. But the trunk is more powerful. It moves ever so slightly when the wind becomes very strong."

"And the root", exclaimed my father, "is the most powerful of all!"

"Yes," his teacher replied. "Already you are seeing the visible/invisible strength of mindfulness. Follow the mindful pathway from blossom to leaf to limb to trunk, and it leads you to the root, the source of the life of the tree. That is Living Meditation demonstrated in daily activity. Where did this root come from, to have so much strength?"

"From a seed?" asked my father timidly.

"Yes. From a mere seed that was part of a leaf cluster. Seed to root to seed again. That is the circle of life. In fact, it is like three circles: You are born with nothing. Everything you own during your lifetime is only temporary. And you take nothing with you when you die except your spirit. You leave behind a good legacy – a good seed."

By this time, the two had reached the top of the hill and were looking back down into the valley.

"What have you learned today?" asked Master Borion.

"I have learned that the root strength is the visible/invisible strength of Living Meditation and of life," replied my father.

"Yes," his teacher nodded. "And if you follow the mindful pathway, you will always come back to the source, to the root. That is the basis of your own strength, your own root. You are human. You are solid. You are steady. You are strong in your potential! Without this power there is no living. And without living there is no power and no hope. For in living, you practice Living Meditation principles to strengthen the root. When you are strong in your centre, you live the correct way. And when you live the correct way, you become strong in your centre. That is balance. That is harmony, which leads to success in life. How do you feel?"

"I feel at peace with this knowledge."

"Good," replied Master Borion. "It is the way of peace. Now let us return to the valley. We have much good to do before the sun will set."

"When can I learn more, teacher?"

"In the next lesson."

The Balance of Knowledge with Wisdom

When we look at the literal meaning of "drunk", we see that it describes someone who has consumed so much alcohol that they cannot speak clearly or behave sensibly. They might also be called foolish, or unwise.

You can borrow knowledge from another person, but not wisdom. Wisdom is all your own, and it must be earned. Over the centuries, the principles of Living Meditation have been passed down to help individuals earn wisdom as they follow the mindful pathway toward strength, peace and happiness.

Confucius spoke a great deal about knowledge and wisdom, and the idea that both are necessary. Like in the yin and yang symbol, balance is essential. It's important in this life to study hard to gain knowledge from books and great teachers. Wisdom, however, can't be acquired in the same way.

Wisdom most often comes with age – although, frankly, I don't think age is the only deciding factor. When you live on this earth for a long time, inevitably you will gain wisdom through experience, but some people may have more wisdom at a much younger age. Experience, it seems, is not the only way to gain wisdom. As Confucius put it, "By three methods, we may learn wisdom: First, by reflection, which is noblest; second, by imitation, which is easiest; and third by experience, which is the bitterest."

So often when we set out to learn something, we use the techniques of memorizing, storing knowledge in our minds. My father would often tell me to stop memorizing.

"Absorb it, munchkin, make it your own," he would say to me.

"What do you mean? Can't I learn everything by memorizing?" I would ask him, puzzled and maybe even a little frustrated.

It took many years for me to truly understand the distinction my father was making between the "head learning", which dominates our academic system, and wisdom, which requires absorbing a way of being. Even now, I can't say "I'm there" and that I have grasped wisdom fully – I believe it's a neverending process. In my life I've been privileged to meet some truly enlightened people, and my father was one of them. These enlightened souls never seem to believe that they have reached the highest point: they keep opening their minds wider, absorbing more. On this, Shakespeare and Confucius agree. The playwright wrote, "The fool doth think he is wise, but the wise man knows himself to be a fool," while the philosopher said, "True wisdom is knowing what you don't know."

Living Meditation is best approached in this way: as something to be absorbed over time. It is not a set of techniques to be memorized, but a way of living to be made your own.

At the end of this mindful pathway is the fulfilment of genuine humanness. I love the word "human". For as long as I can remember I've had this understanding that when you're truly human, you move from your heart. You're grounded. It is a state that brings us together as one, with all of the humans who have come before us, and all who will follow us in the future. To me, it's a deeply connecting concept.

It is possible to lose your humanness. You could say we succumb to a counterfeit or superficial humanness, existing only on the surface. This is where *Doe Chi* comes from: being blind to what is correct, caring little or nothing for the good of others, following an isolated and lonely pathway to nothingness. It sounds terrible, doesn't it? But we see it around us every day. I'd now like to show you the signs of *Doe Chi*, and offer three remedies that can restore our humanness easily, completely and enduringly.

Six Imbalances of *Doe Chi*

Many of us are stuck in today – and I don't mean that in the sense of living in the moment, but in the sense of chasing passing whims and trends. When tomorrow comes we are lost, because we have not built our lives on principles. We have not tapped into the visible/invisible strength of the root. We sway back and forth with every gust of wind. We have no power or peace.

Emotions change all the time. Think of it like this: perhaps you're hot and dehydrated, and you want something to drink. And then the instant you have a cold glass of water, you're no longer thirsty. The feeling disappears. Emotions can be like that. Emotions are clouds passing through the sky. There is nothing wrong with experiencing all emotions, the dark brooding clouds and the white fluffy ones, of course, but we have to acknowledge that they come and go. You may be deeply in love with someone and then, three years down the road, you wake up and find that you simply don't love them anymore. This is not always the way, but we can observe that emotions are a momentary truth while principles endure.

Look around at our society today. On all sides we can see evidence of *Doe Chi*. So many people do not follow principles, but rather pursue their momentary likes and dislikes. Likes and dislikes change constantly, in contrast with principles, which never change. *Doe Chi* is the grand enemy of principles, the adversary of that which is *correct*. Just as a dust storm obscures the vision of the sun, *Doe Chi* obscures the vision of the correct.

Above all, *Doe Chi* is a state of imbalance – too much or too little of something. Here are six of the most common signs of this imbalance. As you read through the signs, take a note of which resonate most with you, or feel familiar to your habits or those around you. If you have a journal, perhaps write down one or two ways you could stop and shift your behaviours in these instances, to help you to move out of *Doe Chi* and into balance.

1. Too Much "True"

You go to dinner with a group of friends. You order pasta. One friend orders a fish main course. Another orders steak. "Why didn't you order the pasta?" you ask your friends. "Pasta is the best choice." They may reply: "Why did you not order fish (or steak)?" Everyone knows what they prefer. Everyone discovers the *true*. But often it is forgotten that another's true may be different from their own.

Quite often an individual compels others to accept their version of the true. Let's say Margot insists, "You must see it my way." But what if her way is not in the best interest of everyone involved? Seeing it Margot's way may seem right to Margot – out of self-interest – but it may not be correct. "You must see it my way" is the voice of *Doe Chi*, and *Doe Chi* is the enemy of the correct. "You must see it my way" has caused an endless array of violence and war throughout history. Look around you: everyone discovers their true, but very few discover the correct.

2. Too Much "Right"

Do you see people insisting that their way of doing things is the *right* way, even though it may not serve the greater good of all involved? Have you seen parents driving themselves relentlessly toward a goal, to the neglect of their families? Let's say Carl declares, "I must reach the top of my industry and make my fortune. I am doing it for my family." In reality Carl may be shortening his life and denying his family a true lasting legacy. "I must prove myself at all costs" – that is the voice of *Doe Chi*. To view things solely in the duality of "right" and "wrong", we disregard the vast space in between. The ancient symbol of yin and yang shows us that in dark, there is always some light; and in light, there is always some darkness. Absolutes are rarely the path to wise decisions. In such drunkenness, we gamble with the opportunities that belong to those who follow a mindful pathway. *Doe Chi* is stubborn and selfish. Being stuck on what is true or right, *Doe Chi* never arrives at what is correct.

3. Too Much Not Knowing

What if we do not understand the principle of the Way of True-Right-Correct? More than that, what if we don't *want* to understand? Worst of all, what if we don't even *know* we don't know? What if we are stuck in the passive mode of ignorance and just accept someone else's opinion of what is true and right – and so never arrive at correct on our own? What if we bend like the limbs and leaves of the tree with every gust of wind?

It is easy to say, "They told me what to do." This kind of drunkenness – *Doe Chi* – is lazy and listless, resisting principle and genuine strength. In today's world, we are pressed from every side with other people's opinions – often presented as facts – and it is easier to remain passive than to seek the correct.

4. Too Much Blame

Wesley returns home from work and ignores his wife's request to help with the children. "You don't understand how difficult my day has been," he says. "I need to relax and watch TV. I'm right. You are wrong." Any time you hear the words, "You don't understand how I feel", you are very likely hearing the voice of *Doe Chi*. Maybe you know the saying, "When you point one finger, there are three fingers pointing back to you." *Doe Chi* blames others in order to release its own pain. As a result, *Doe Chi* ends up alone.

"It's your fault" is a road sign along the blind and careless pathway. That pathway leads to false humanness because it destroys harmony and peace.

5. Too Much Failure

"I've tried so hard to change all my life, but it never works. I always stay the same." That is one of the many voices of *Doe Chi*. It denies the Living Meditation principle: you can change your own reality. If you have business problems, you are in control of how you respond to them and you can change them. If you have relationship problems, you are in control of how you respond to them and you can change them. True humanity is self-made. You can achieve it by following principles, by tapping into the root of genuine power, by travelling the mindful pathway. When you follow principles, you train your mind; you build courage and realize the power YOU have to change your circumstances.

As I write this, my son is learning to play golf, and I'm finding that it is such an incredible sport to have in children's lives. In golf, you can be on a winning streak, then you take just one bad putt and the game is lost. His golf lessons have given us an opportunity to talk about failure and what it truly means. I love the advice from Phil Kenyon, a putting coach, who says that one of the biggest errors amateur golfers make is believing that you are either a good or a bad putter. I tell my son that you can't get stuck in the idea of failure: instead, you can believe in your ability to change circumstances. Don't limit yourself with your current beliefs.

6. Too Much Self-Pride

"Why are you always criticizing me? Mind your own business." That is the voice of *Doe Chi*. *Doe Chi* rejects criticism and suggestions. It says, "I don't care how I look. I don't care how I live. I don't care about tomorrow." *Doe Chi* cannot see in other people the desire to help and improve because it becomes immune to deep love and friendship. *Doe Chi* has self-interest, but not self-awareness. *Doe Chi* is blind to family and community bonds. *Doe Chi* has ears stopped up with self-pride. *Doe Chi* has a heart hardened by ego.

This is not to say we should listen to every random stranger shouting criticism about how you dress or walk or drive. The people closest to me, who see me and love me, may not always be correct but I will naturally be more open to their advice. We can be open to listening, but it doesn't mean we must heed everything blindly – that would be an excess of absorption, not the balanced intake of wisdom we talked about earlier. By opening ourselves up to the way a loved one may see our situation, it gives us the opportunity (though not the obligation) to see ourselves and our circumstances from another perspective.

Three Remedies for Being Drunk on Your Own Thoughts

1. Open Up Your Inner Eye

Your outer eye sees the fluttering leaves and the swaying branches. It focuses on fleeting likes and dislikes. Your inner eye sees the root and focuses on principles. So, tap into the visible/invisible strength. Choose genuine humanness as your goal. Look for the good, the noble, the enduring; then you will find that the correct will become visible to you each day. You will know your true self and make an alliance with destiny as you journey along the mindful path.

As you follow your heart and the Way of True-Right-Correct, the noise of *Doe Chi* will give way to the peaceful quiet of deep power and lasting harmony.

2. Cultivate Genuine Relationships

The strongest sword is made of tempered steel that has been subjected to intense pressure and heat again and again, until it is nearly indestructible. In the same way, a genuine relationship tempers your mind again and again until it becomes strong and resilient. Genuine relationships can be had with people who point out a negative quality to help you grow; they help you gain perspective – to zoom out. Be grateful for genuine criticism from those you trust. Consider it an act of loyalty and love, of genuine friendship and compassion.

Suppose your spouse or your best friend points out a deficiency in you. Maybe it's something simple like suggesting you wear a different outfit for a specific event, or your habit of talking on your phone in a crowded movie theatre. Maybe it is something more serious, like your dismissive attitude about your parents' sincere concern for your wellbeing. Understand where they are coming from. What they are really saying is, "I am interested in you. I am interested in your wellbeing. I am someone who loves you; therefore, I am telling you something I believe would be in your best interest for the given situation." They are acting on the principle of a genuine relationship. Look for this principle, and make the correct decision based on principle. What happens when you do that? You improve! You learn from your loved ones! You become more aware, and you are grateful.

True relationships are based on loyalty. Because loyalty is a principle, it never changes. Likes and dislikes can change with the moment, but your spouse or best friend is being loyal. You cannot buy loyalty; it must be earned. In the Korean business world, managers use a process of gradually letting you see your faults. Your manager tells you nine things you did right, then one thing you did wrong. True and deep relationships never use this method. Someone who cares about you will tell you nine things that you can improve upon and one thing you did well, with the intention of always helping you to become that much better. The concept might seem extreme, but when you have built up genuine trust in a relationship, you can pave over the detour of insecurities – the six imbalances of *Doe Chi* – and accept observations, which you can use as a strength to see yourself and your reality more clearly.

That is a genuine relationship. It says, "I am interested in helping you move forward along the mindful pathway."

Do not expect *constant* grand gestures of approval from your spouse or friends. Do not look for flowery compliments at all times, but make sure you genuinely savour and appreciate kind, loving words when they are spoken. Genuine friends show their approval in subtle and quiet ways. A discreet nod, a silent look. You learn the signals. *Doe Chi* is noisy and boisterous. Genuine relationships do not cultivate *Doe Chi*, but rather the deep and silent strength of love and empathy. Spouses learn over the years to express their approval in invisible ways that come not just through words, but are expressed as subtle gestures from the heart. Marriage partners learn over the years to express their approval in invisible ways that come from the heart, not the tongue. With genuine relationships all around you, you will find that the clamour and show of *Doe Chi* will fade. In its place you will have security in the enduring strength of the root.

3. Move Your Chi

When your body is stagnant, your chi – your life force – becomes stagnant. When your chi becomes stagnant, your mind becomes stagnant. Our mind and body are interconnected, so stagnant chi in the body ultimately deeply affects the mind. Very often when we feel uptight it can be caused by chi stagnation. When our minds and bodies become stressed, our chi becomes imbalanced and does not flow properly. You can literally feel it if you check into your body – pain, fatigue, tightness, for example. The simplest way to rebalance this is to move.

Common exercises, like brisk walking, running, CrossFit or interval training, get our blood moving and help to break up stagnation. As so many of us sit down for a lot of our day, whether that's at work, in the car or on the sofa catching up on Netflix – we forget that our bodies were designed for movement. We need to move regularly throughout the day to stimulate our energies and brain like a key in an ignition. It doesn't have to be "exercise", just movement. So consider how you can break up your day with more regular movement. Even just getting up and walking around your desk every hour is beneficial.

Beyond this, there is a reason that breathwork practices, traditional yoga and certain traditional martial arts, like Tai Chi and Qi (Chi) Gong, have been handed down for millennia. These practices are extremely effective ways to improve circulation, strengthen organ systems, relieve tension and open the meridian systems, so that chi can flow freely through the body.

When I first asked my father how to meditate, he told me to sit down with my back straight, relax my body, breathe into my nose to the top of my head, down my spine, into my abdomen and out of my mouth. Then ask myself, *Who am I? Why I am here? What is my purpose?* For him, meditation was as simple – and as profound – as that.

Often, we think of movement and meditation as separate practices, but one of the methods that has been handed down in my lineage is to combine movement with meditation. Immediately, or shortly after your physical practice or exercise, you sit for your meditation. Because some days are packed with meetings, children or other work, I may only have time for five minutes of movement and seven minutes of meditation. But cultivating the practice of getting regular movement into your schedule helps to clear stagnation and build the free flow of chi for your body and mind so that you can take on the day with more clarity and energy.

One simple Qi Gong or "moving meditation" exercise that can be done anywhere and at any time is called *Separating Heaven and Earth*. This exercise can quickly rebalance the body and calm the mind, help to improve digestion and increase circulation, as well as benefit the heart and immediately relieve stress. Physically, it also helps to strengthen and lengthen the muscles of the arms, shoulders, back and abdomen.

1. To do this exercise, stand with your feet comfortably apart, about the width of your shoulders or slightly wider. Your arms should be relaxed next to your body with your palms toward your legs. This is your basic neutral stance.
2. Next, breathe out from your abdomen as you reach up with one arm (palm facing toward the sky), while lowering the other (palm facing toward the earth). Keep a soft curve in both arms.
3. Breathe in as you bring your arms back to chest level and breathe out as you swap arms, one going high and the other low.
4. Finish the movement by inhaling as you bring your palms toward your chest, arms bent as if you are hugging a barrel (picture bringing energy from the universe into your heart and chest).
5. Then, breathe out as you turn your palms toward the ground and lower them, as if you are pushing the energy from your hands into the ground.
6. Repeat the exercise for 3–5 minutes.

"Just as you may not see clearly if you are drunk from alcohol, you can also be so "drunk" on your own thoughts that you can't see your surroundings clearly anymore. In order to see life more clearly ... zoom out."

KEY FOUR: HOW WILL YOU BE REMEMBERED?

I often reflect upon this question.

One day, when I am gone from this world, you may not remember my face, you may not remember my name, but it is my true wish that I leave something behind that will have made a difference, that will have made this world better and more positive.

This thought is what drives me in this life; it is my spark, you might say. As human beings, we all need to have a spark to help us through challenging times, or times when we feel stuck – something that will catapult us out of that sticky spot. For me, it is this concept of planting good seeds that will bear fruit (or positivity) for future generations through our intentions and, ultimately, our actions.

In Korean culture, our ancestors matter deeply to us. We observe rituals by which we remember them, demonstrating that those who have passed from this life are never truly departed from our hearts. In the same way, we consider our descendants and what spiritual legacy we are handing down to them. Just as our ancestors influence our lives, we will continue to serve the generations that come after us.

Through this understanding and way of living comes a deep sense of purpose, regardless of your specific belief systems.

If each one of us is mindful of the seeds that we are planting along our journey, we will truly make a difference for our children and all of the generations to come.

This is how we can leave a legacy of goodness.

At noon, Master Borion and my father were seated on a flat rock ledge near a flowing mountain stream. Far below them, the citizens of the valley were cultivating their farms and gardens in the heat of the day. Above them, an eagle traced a spiral in the cloudless sky.

"How dark it is today," remarked Master Borion. "I will light a candle and send illumination into the world." And he took a candle from his bag and carefully lit it, shielding it from the breeze.

Surprised, my father shielded his eyes from the sun and looked toward his teacher with anticipation.

"Where is the darkest place?" asked Master Borion. "Where is the candle needed most?"

My father glanced about him. "Over there, perhaps, in the shadow of that oak tree?"

Master Borion said nothing.

"Or over there," added my father, "where that cave leads into the mountain?"

"Where is the closest, tightest place?" asked Master Borion. "That is where this candle is most needed."

My father was lost for words.

"You look all around you for darkness," said his teacher, "but you forget to look toward yourself. Beneath you, under you, between yourself and the rock where you sit – that is the darkest place. That is the closest, tightest place. That is where the candle is needed."

"The light of self-knowledge?" whispered my father.

"Yes," replied Master Borion. "Look down there at all those workers in the valley. They labour to support their families and that is a correct thing to do. But they labour in blindness. They do not see the darkness under their own feet. And when the time comes for them to die and go the way of all flesh, what do they leave behind?"

"Their farms, their homes," said my father.

"And after a time, who remembers them for these material things? What is the legacy they leave behind for their families?"

At this my father could think of nothing to say.

"Are you hungry?" asked Master Borion.

"Oh, yes!" responded my father, eagerly.

"What do you see here?" asked his teacher, pulling an object from a container in his bag. "Are you hungry for this?"

My father recoiled in horror at the sight of a bruised and rotten apple.

"Rotten fruit," said Master Borion.

"Rotten fruit," echoed my father, pulling back. "What for?"

"What for, indeed," Master Borion nodded. "So many people leave a legacy for their families of rotten fruit. When they die, they leave behind them no good seeds for the next generation. Into the world they come with nothing. They gather up material goods for a time. And then they leave – with nothing. They see the world around them, but never themselves. They are quick to find fault with their neighbour, but overlook the darkness within themselves. They have no earnings."

"No earnings?" asked my father, puzzled.

"There are only two types of riches for humans," replied Master Borion. "Visible riches and invisible riches. We have visible riches for only a short time, but invisible riches last forever. The invisible riches come from being an honourable role model. Those are our earnings, our legacy. It is the invisible riches that are our good seed. This good seed will help others, who will in turn help still others. These invisible riches will multiply and grow. This is the principle of success in human life. These riches can be attained when people overcome the darkness within themselves."

"But how can they change?"

"By opening up their invisible eye. In this life we hold the choice. Seeing the mindful path requires looking in faith and wisdom with the invisible eye. Long before we were born, this path has existed. The visible eye too easily follows the material way. The invisible eye follows the principle, the Way of True-Right-Correct along the mindful pathway."

"How can I make sure the fruit doesn't spoil?" asked my father.

"Movement."

"Movement?"

"Moving waters do not go stagnant or spoil. Moving waters are constantly being refreshed. See this stream. It remains fresh and pure by moving along its course of destiny toward the ocean."

"But, Master," objected my father. "You once said that moving water speaks with the noisy voice of Doe Chi, *of selfishness."*

"All of nature teaches the lesson you look for," replied Master Borion. "Look carefully at this cascading stream. It bubbles and tumbles, but along the cascade are many pools. Each pool is deep and calm. Nevertheless, the water in each pool moves."

"The pools seem to be at rest," said my father.

"But they move with invisible movement, like a person agile with self-knowledge. Moving waters do not stagnate. Your life is like this deep moving water. Selfishness is rotten. Being drunk with material things is rotten. Moving water endures. A legacy lives on forever. What do you see up there?"

My father gazed at the sky above them. "I see the eagle circling."

"Indeed. The eagle moves slowly, gracefully, surely. The eagle teaches humanness at its root centre. Between the clouds and the sky is the realm of humanness. Look for yourself in that place. Look with the invisible eye. Leave behind you a legacy of balance, harmony, peace, joy and strength. Be such a person. When such a person walks along the pathway, his

presence is felt there forever. That is their legacy. That is the good fruit with the good seed."

With that, Master Borion handed the candle to my father and said, "It is your destiny to send illumination into the world. That is your hunger. That is your mission. Are you truly hungry?"

My father did not dare to respond to this question, thinking of the rotten apple in his teacher's bag.

Master Borion smiled. "There are two hungers," he said, "the invisible hunger for the enduring legacy, and the visible hunger for essential food. Come, let us go down and pick some fresh apples in the valley."

At that, my father was relieved. He smiled. He understood. "How can I be more like you, Grand Master?"

"In the next lesson you will learn," replied Master Borion.

The Light Inside You

A thought that resonates with me deeply is that all of the answers in this life can be found within ourselves and within the natural world around us. It is a thought that might seem a little uncomfortable at first. "*Everything is inside of me* – what does that even mean?" But there is a balance to be found here. We are all connected, but the place to begin finding answers is within ourselves.

In Living Meditation, everything points back to our inner being. We are the ones who choose what to do in this life: whether to *respond* or *react*, whether we make a stand or sit back silently. So many of us think that we have to look outward to find the answer – to find God, to find faith – but truly, it all starts from within. I see this principle playing out in all religions, all forms of spirituality and faith.

Humanness loves light. Humanness sees the light in others and feels driven to help them find more of it. But at the end of the day, no one can light you up except yourself. You can have incredible mentors, you can be surrounded by people you love, you can have amazing experiences – these are all good things. Ultimately, though, it is up to you to light the candle of self-knowledge within yourself.

How do you feel? You can touch yourself and know that you exist. With your outer eye, you can see your hands, your body and your visible self. But can you see the invisible self? Can you open the invisible eye and see the heart, the true self and the root of your being? Are you light or darkness? Is there darkness in you that needs to be filled with illumination? If you can see the invisible self with the invisible eye, then you see the legacy that you will leave behind when you depart from this life.

The candle is needed in the darkest place. That place is not outside, but close to you and even within you. Best of all, once you illuminate yourself, you can illuminate the pathway for the people you love.

Your Legacy

It can be so important for us to keep in mind that material things do not endure. We come into this world with nothing, then for a time we temporarily gather our visible things, but these do not endure. When we leave, we leave behind all of these material and physical "things". Such things that belong to this earth, belong to this earth – we cannot take them with us.

It is fine to possess material things: houses, cars, cosy chairs and soft blankets can make for a more comfortable daily life for you and your loved ones. Always remember, though, that while you can own material things, material things can also own you – if you let them.

"We come into this world with nothing, then for a time we temporarily gather our visible things, but these do not endure. When we leave, we leave behind all of these material and physical "things". Such things that belong to this earth, belong to this earth – we cannot take them with us."

Consider the 5–10 things that are the most important to you in your life.

What enriches your life, what do you love the most?
Write them down.
Have a look at the list. What, and who, is on there?
This can be a profound lesson in the importance of the "things" we surround ourselves with.

Many of us strive to create a legacy for our children, but often in our minds it is solely the financial one we're concerned with. We can become very stressed if we are not able to make that kind of material provision in the way we would like. But there is a more significant, more enduring legacy we can provide for our children and families, which is a spiritual one.

Such a legacy is built up through small actions: treating others well, being kind, looking out for our colleagues and neighbours. These acts may seem small, but they are like seeds. When it is first planted, a seed is a tiny thing. Over time a seed grows into a fragrant plant or a beautiful vine or a mighty tree – it is genuinely hard to imagine that the tallest of rainforest trees still grows from a tiny seed. It becomes more than it was when it began. The good seed endures and spreads hope, resilience and strength to the next generation.

When I was young and my father first told me the story about the rotting fruit, I was shocked. "Ew! Why are you telling me about a rotten apple?" It certainly made an impression on me! My father explained to me that rotten fruit is not all bad: the apple that drops from the tree returns to the earth and breaks down to enrich the soil for a fuller unfolding of life later on.

The principles of Living Meditation have been passed down over the centuries as a bond to preserve families. One of life's purposes is to pass on to our children and our community a good role model that shows how these principles enable us to achieve balance, harmony, strength and peace.

If you were to die tomorrow, how would you be remembered? Would they say, "That person was excellent at their job"? Or, "I never saw much of them – they kept to themselves"? Or would they say, "That person was kind, a good example for their children and community, someone who showed empathy and exemplified how to live in balance and harmony"? Your family will be left with the visible things you have gathered together, but these will not lead to an enduring legacy. They can bring ease and comfort in the short term, which is important while we live in this reality, but when we depart this reality they fade away like the petals of a flower. The good seeds, however, are enduring lessons of positivity, compassion, empathy, courage, character and consistency, and they have the potential to grow and meaningfully provide for the next generation.

As a parent, I take the idea of a spiritual legacy very seriously, and it is so rewarding when I get a glimpse that the seeds are taking root. The other day I was with my sons out in the courtyard, and Jackson said to me, "I can't wait to go to the lab with you one day."

"That's great, Jackson, but why do you want to come with me?"

"I want to help you and Daddy at the lab and do good things," my three-year-old told me solemnly.

What an awesome thing to hear him say. So often we tell our boys, "This is why Mommy does this, or why Daddy behaves this way. You know what your grandma is like, and this is what your papa did too. We try to do good things and be kind to others, because that is how we leave good seeds for the future."

Open up your inner eye. What do you see yourself giving to your family? What lessons do you act out for them on the stage of life? What light do you shed on the pathway your family is to follow? You can give them material gifts and comforts to add variety and joy to life, but these will fade eventually. The spiritual gifts that nurture self-respect and compassion toward others, however – these will endure.

The Flow of Moving Water

It is important to keep in mind that life is an ever-flowing and ever-changing cycle, and by holding on too tightly we can break the connection. Through this connection we "plug in" to a wavelength, an energy, a flow of life that we are all a part of. This is the Tao.

The Tao is all about flow: moving with the flow and having a deep awareness of all that flows around us. When we are in the flow, we gain perspective and see things clearly in a way that isn't possible when we are still and stagnant. Good physical health is all about flow, too. Within our bodies, we experience wellness when our organs, our muscles, our joints and our circulation are functioning properly. The cells are nourished and waste is eliminated; nothing remains static. The same thing is true in other aspects of life: we have to go with the flow, moving in its rhythm, never getting stuck in one place, otherwise, we are like stagnant water that spoils and turns toxic, unable to sustain life.

Here is another thought about moving water. Where does the good seed flourish? Near flowing streams of deep water. Where is the moving water? It is in those homes where principle and heart combine to teach togetherness, love, generosity and the joy of staying resolute on the good pathway.

Principle and heart go together. You can look at your children and your family members in two ways: with heart and with principle. When you see them with principle, you look at them as if they were trees. Principle is constant, strong, deeply rooted. When you look at your family members with your heart, you look at them as growing, beautiful individuals who are becoming truly human.

There is a time for principle. There is a time for heart. To look at children with both principle and heart is to leave behind a legacy of wisdom and faith – the good seed of balance, harmony, strength, peace and joy.

Let's say you give a child an apple. That is a gift of the heart. The apple gives momentary joy and keeps the child satisfied for an hour. Then the child asks for more, so you give the child a carton of apples. But that is neither an act of the heart, nor an act of principle. It is not even rational.

The act of principle is to teach the child to *grow apple trees* (or, in our modern world, perhaps to earn money to buy their own apples). The child may resist learning the work of growing apple trees, but principle doesn't give way to excuses or the easy way out. The parent sees through their invisible eye the child growing up and being able to enjoy apples for a lifetime. The heart delights in this view, and principle is preserved on the child's behalf.

Another example comes from my own home not so long ago. Vince came home from school and told me he had gotten in trouble for talking in class. "Mommy, I'm sorry, but here's how it happened." He tells me his story about why he was talking – it made perfect sense to him and he felt it was unfair that he was punished. My heart wants to say, "Oh, Vince, I get it. It's okay." All I want to do is hug him and tell him that I wish his teacher saw the whole situation. But no matter how much I want to move from my heart in that moment, this is where principle comes in. I have to teach my son that no matter what his reasoning might be, when you are in class you cannot be disruptive. As Vince's parent it is my duty to teach him the correct thing, versus being led by my heart.

The heart and principle working together – that is wisdom, and it will lead us to the correct decision.

The Eight Keys

Heart and principle working together are like faith plus wisdom. Faith is using your invisible eye to see yourself and your loved ones in a state of true humanness. Wisdom is making correct choices in the spirit of faith and hope. Faith and wisdom are deep water that is moving and never stagnates.

Look around you at all the challenges and opportunities of life. Each one is different. Each one has its own door. In this book we talk about the eight keys of Living Meditation. Each one will open doors for you, and if you have faith and wisdom, you can open every door.

Each of the eight keys will help you achieve the legacy you can leave behind for your children and the coming generations. It is the good seed for which you will never be forgotten.

How can we understand and apply the eight keys? We have to look inside ourselves – but also to the universe all around us. The universe offers us many models and mirrors and ways of understanding. Start with yourself, then look outward. Keep moving, keep checking in with yourself and then with the universe. This is the kind of movement, the kind of practice, that never stops and never stagnates but sustains life within us and all around us; this is Living Meditation.

KEY FIVE: SEEK CONNECTEDNESS & HONOUR

The wisdom of the ages, revealed through different philosophies and faith traditions, shows one fundamental truth: that all things are connected and strength comes from the root.

The highest good in life is to follow the way of connectedness to others, to your surroundings and to your ultimate being.

Even in our modern times, connectedness is often spoken of as a virtue, a goal to strive for. But we don't hear so much about honour anymore. It seems an outdated concept, bringing to mind medieval images of knights and duels, jousting and damsels in distress. But in East Asian wisdom and culture, honour is very much alive and present in a way that is not seen so strongly in Western culture. Think of *Bushido*, the code that all members of Japan's Samurai class were obliged to follow. A little like the European notion of chivalry, it required warriors to follow principles of loyalty and duty. *Bushido* later became the basis for the teaching of ethics in Japan, with principles that still remain relevant today.

On first glance, we may not identify with these ancient warriors. But consider what "warrior" represents in yoga. If you practise yoga, you will be familiar with Virabhadrasana or warrior pose. It is a standing pose that helps build focus, power and stability. Now, these are qualities that we can strive for – even if we don't see ourselves as modern-day warriors! I want to show you how honour, too, is relevant to our lives today.

But first, what *is* honour?

A person of honour is a role model of connectedness on the path of goodness. Honour is driven by love and sustained through respect. True honour means respecting the light in others.

Honour means living in such a way that you pass on good seeds to your children and the coming generations. Honour preserves the connection to the root, the source of enduring strength and vitality. Honour overcomes the forces of greed, envy, selfishness, anger and prejudice. Honour produces harmony, balance, peace and joy.

In life there are always circumstances that will challenge our honour. A friend criticizes you behind your back; your spouse complains about the amount of time you spend on a hobby; you have a business opportunity that could make you a fortune, but to other peoples' detriment. What does honour look like in this moment?

"Honour is driven by love and sustained through respect."

The sun was just rising as Master Borion and my father began walking down the hill toward the village. In the distance, the rosy glow of morning touched the mountain's snowy peak.

"How beautiful," remarked my father. "The mountain presents many faces. Sometimes it is pink, like this morning, then in the evening it is red. In the moonlight it is grey and against the starry sky it is black."

"Many expressions, but one face," replied Master Borion.

"How so?"

"The mountain is the mountain," responded his teacher. "It is always the same. The mountain has the face of honour. What face do you have?"

My father silently touched his own cheek.

"Look at me," said Master Borion. "What do you see?"

"I see the face of wisdom."

"And?"

"The face of kindness."

"And?"

"The face of peace."

"And?"

"The face of strength."

"How many faces do you see?"

"Four," answered my father, somewhat bewildered.

"Count again," insisted Master Borion.

Then my father understood. "Master, I see one face – the face of honour."

Master Borion smiled. "It is very important to have one face."

By now, the two had entered the village. Many people were rushing about at the start of the workday. Master Borion pointed to a bench beneath an oak tree near the market square. There they sat down to observe the people.

"So many faces," said Master Borion. "Do you see their faces?"

"Yes, I see many faces," confirmed my father.

"Many visible faces," said Master Borion. "But in many cases their true faces are invisible – hidden by masks."

"Masks?" questioned my father. "I see no masks."

"The key is the eyes," responded his teacher. "The eyes are the windows of the true face. See that woman over there holding her newborn child? What do you see in her eyes?"

"I see peace."

"Yes. She is a traveller on the mindful pathway. She aspires to a face of honour. The face of honour has eyes of peace. She has a vision of leaving good seeds behind for her child. What do you see over there?"

My father looked in the direction of a villager in fine clothing, strutting proudly across the square. "I see a wealthy man," he said, "perhaps the wealthiest in the village. Look, he is giving a coin to that beggar."

"You see a mask," said Master Borion. "His true face is not visible."

"He seems rather sure of himself."

"He deceives himself," Master Borion replied. "He thinks he has the face of power and wealth, but that is a mask. He thinks he can wear the face of charity, but that too is a mask, for he has gained his wealth by stealing from others. His eyes are the eyes of greed. He pretends to wear the face of honour, but in fact he has no face at all. He travels a blind and careless pathway. He leaves behind no good seeds."

"Can people like that change their masks to fit the occasion?" asked my father.

"Dishonour has many faces, many masks," responded Master Borion. "But wearing masks always has consequences. Masks can cause great damage to the individual and to others. A mask lives only for the present, leaving no good seed. A face of honour lives forever. Finding your one true face, the face of honour – that is the highest form of humanness."

Just then two young men walked up and sat down on an adjacent bench to talk. One wore a red shirt, the other blue.

"Listen carefully," Master Borion instructed my father quietly.

"It's good to see you again," said the man in the red shirt to his companion. "I missed you while you were travelling. We were always such close friends."

After the two had exchanged warm compliments and renewed their friendship for a few minutes, the man in blue bid his friend farewell and walked over to a nearby shop.

"They wear the face of friendship and honour," remarked my father.

"Wait and see," said Master Borion.

Presently a young woman walked up and sat down next to the man in red.

"I see your friend has returned from his trip," she said.

"Yes."

"I often wondered about him," she continued. "He's always so happy and cheerful, but I think it's all an act. None of us ever really trusted him."

"Exactly," agreed the man in red. "He always had it so easy. Always the lucky one. Always thought he was so good. But he's such a pain!"

My father glanced at Master Borion in surprise.

"What do you see?" asked Master Borion quietly.

"I understand now," replied my father. "The man in red has two faces."

"Only two?" asked his teacher. "Where there are two, there are more. Here is a riddle: What has a thousand faces and yet no face?"

"Dishonour," my father answered.

"Yes," said Master Borion. "In dishonour there is no true face, only masks and self-deception. Remember, having no face is having no honour. Without honour there are no friends; with honour, true friends abound."

Moments later, the young man in red stood up, said goodbye to the young woman, and disappeared into the crowd. After a few minutes the young man in blue returned, carrying a bundle of fresh fruit.

"Hello," he said to the young woman. "It's good to see you again. I was just talking to ..."

"Yes," she interrupted. "He left for an appointment, thank heavens."

"What do you mean?" asked the man in blue.

"He's such a snake!" she exclaimed. "He's no good at all."

"Stop!" said the young man. "He is my friend and I won't hear you saying wrong about him."

"Some friend," she replied. "You should have heard the bad things he said about you behind your back."

"If that is the case," responded the young man, "then I would prefer to hear those things from him directly. As his friend, I owe him that much. He remains my friend until he proves otherwise." With that, the young man in blue nodded goodbye and departed quickly.

"What do you see now?" asked Master Borion.

"I see the man in blue has face. He is an honourable man. The others have masks, but no face. Face is honour. I, too, want the face of honour."

"And if you have such a face," asked Master Borion, "when will you show it?"

"I will show that same face always," said my father.

"That is correct," his teacher replied. "You will show the face of honour to your friends, to your family, to everyone. That is the face you will pass on to your next generation, the face of honour. You will do this because you are the mountain and the mountain does not change. You are deep moving water that remains fresh and pure. You are the eagle that circles high above the clouds. You are the traveller below on the mindful pathway."

"Teacher, how can I be like you?"

"Open the invisible eye," said Master Borion. "See your true self unfolding. Go with destiny by changing your reality."

"How can I change my reality?" asked my father, puzzled.

"With the next lesson, we shall see," replied Master Borion, who was already striding away from the crowd.

Honour is Connection

All things are connected. Strength comes from the root, for the root endures. From the root flows the life of the individual, family, community, nation and world. To be connected to the root is life. To be separated from the root is death. We can see that the highest good in life is to follow the way of connectedness, and pass on good seeds to the coming generations.

Honour is a central principle of Living Meditation. The person who demonstrates connectedness on the mindful pathway is a person of honour. When I think about honour, I think about qualities like integrity and character.

Here is a way to think of it. The meaning of honour is to pass good seeds on to your children and coming generations. It connects us even more widely, with all of nature and all of the human beings who have come before us and those who are yet to come. The power behind honour is love – love of your family and your children, your community and all people. The fruits of honour are harmony, balance, peace and joy.

The opposite of honour is dishonour. The greatest dishonour in life is to withhold good seeds from your family and the generations to come, either through action or lack of action. Either way, the result is that others are denied harmony, balance, peace, joy and external and internal strength. Such a denial breaks the connection and brings a separation from the root.

Some spiritual teachers say that the primary motivating force behind dishonour is hate. But this word "hate" is so strong, so powerful, I don't like to use it. I don't even let my young sons say it because there is so much negativity in this word and rarely does the way we use it warrant such intensity. Instead of hatred, my father would talk to me about blindness. How is it possible, he would ask me, for individuals to be blind to their own family, their own children and other people? Some people, he explained, can be said to be blind to their family and others because they sacrifice wellbeing – their own and that of those around them – for wealth, power and pride. The craving for such material and temporary things is the calling of *Doe Chi* – being drunk with one's own thoughts and words.

Then there are other people who seek honour without connectedness, without love. Instead, they seek honour in visible things. More than that, they seek honour in tearing down rather than building up, breaking apart rather than connecting, serving self rather than serving others. Such people have no face because they have no honour. Instead, they wear a false face, a mask. In fact, they have many masks: one for each person they meet, one for each occasion in life. They are denying their humanness. Such counterfeit humanness has a thousand faces and yet no face at all.

In the story of the mountain, Master Borion taught my father about having face. This is something our society today definitely understands and we see it in phrases like "being two-faced". We see politicians being two-faced when they are not steadfast in their beliefs but change their position according to what will benefit them the most in any given situation. This is different from being flexible, where you are grounded in principle and mindfully go with the flow. When you are two-faced, you are not grounded – not connected – at all.

By way of contrast, humanness in its highest form has only one face and no masks. It has the same face of honour for all occasions, and for all people and for all time. To find your own true face of honour is to bring about connectedness, to connect with the coming generations through good seeds. Such connectedness, such honour, comes about through love.

Two Kinds of Blindness

There are two kinds of blindness: blindness based on greed, and blindness based on ignorance. To look for the easy way in life is the way of greed. That form of blindness says, "These other people have what I want, so I'm going to take it from them. To take it from them, I must declare these people to have no value. Since they have no value, I can rob them." Internet fraud and elder abuse are two extreme examples of this kind of blindness, though it shows itself in more subtle ways too, like envying your neighbour for their big house and brand-new car or devaluing a colleague because of their race. But this is the voice of *Doe Chi*. It is spoken by a mask, by someone with no true self. It is self-deception because it masks the truth. The truth is that when we behave in this way, we cut ourselves off from our own potential greatness.

The other form of blindness is based on ignorance: not knowing one's true self, or, worse, *not knowing that one does not know*. That phrase is like a tongue twister or a riddle, but it simply means that we don't know we're doing the wrong thing. I have always believed that most people don't set out to do bad things. Most people pursue their path thinking they are doing the right thing. Without knowing our true selves, we are blinded by ignorance. Hiding behind the mask of ignorance, we say, "I do not know my true self and I am not worth knowing. What I do not know, I cannot love. That is why I must wear the mask of ignorance – to cover the shame of the truth." A lack of self-confidence is a symptom of this kind of blindness. When we are stuck in ignorance, we can't pass down any good seeds. We are broken off from the true root. We have no honour and therefore no face. You can see how important it is to know your true self and to find the face of honour.

Greed and ignorance make us blind and, when we are blind, we are not in touch. We are not connected. We lose perspective and we even start to lose ourselves.

Lift Others Up

When you are on a mindful pathway, you find honour by lifting others up. The parent lifts the child. The teacher lifts the student. The friend lifts the friend. How do you lift others up? Through the power of respect. True respect means honouring the light in others. You honour the light in others by helping them connect to the root of strength and purpose. Respect means being a good role model. True respect means planting seeds of harmony, balance, peace and joy.

There is no respect in forcing others to change or in doing for them something they should learn to do for themselves. That would deprive them of the opportunity to learn the Way of True-Right-Correct. Rather, respect means lifting others up – often simply by being an example – to open their invisible eye and see themselves in their true light as the highest form of humanness. When they see themselves in this true light, they desire to choose the correct, for the fruits of this pathway become sweet and delicious to them.

Honour means respecting others in the role they perform for the good of all. Consider a house. The main beam of the framework supports the whole house. When the window does not fit securely and the winds and rains come in, the main beam doesn't leave its place to become the window. If that were to happen, the whole house would fall. Similarly, the door does not become the wall, nor the wall the ceiling. Rather, all are connected together and each plays its essential role. The same principle applies to the family, where the parents support the whole but still show respect for each child by allowing him or her to learn honour in playing a role suited to their age and ability. The parents respect the light in each other and in each child and, by doing so cultivate balance, sharing, love and mutual respect.

This image is an important one for me. When I picture this house, I see my father as the foundation and myself as one of the pillars. But in my visualization, this house grows and changes. Over time, I become the foundation and my children become the pillars. We respect the light in each other and the role we each play. And there isn't just one house; there are many, all interconnected, like those beautiful villages in Greece where white-washed houses rise up from the seaside in one magnificent whole.

Invisible Harm

What is it that is missing in our modern world? I believe it is a fundamental sense of connectedness. The family is under siege from the forces of separation, of breaking apart, of being disconnected from the root. Many of us are working harder and have less time together as a family. Through the pandemic of 2020–21 we all felt isolated from our friends and family, and it has been hard for many to recover a sense of intimacy and connection.

Honour grows with great difficulty in the rocky seedbed of material excess. Respect struggles to survive in an atmosphere of greed and selfishness. But the greatest harm from being disconnected from the root is invisible, because it happens within. Being separated from the root brings inner doubt and insecurity. Doubt and insecurity cover the face of the true self and create a hunger for external masks.

The modern world is populated with the distorted masks of greed, envy, selfishness, anger and prejudice. These masks stare out with the eyes of blindness and destruction, but the blindness and destruction also work within to scar the soul. Greed consumes the heart a little at a time, until the heart dies. Envy kills self-confidence and initiative with the flattering lie that what others have earned you can seize with no effort on your part. Selfishness will steal another's honour, but the selfish individual really steals only from themself by denying their own self-worth and potential. Anger destroys balance and harmony and disrupts the Way of True-Right-Correct. Prejudice violates love by stealing away the worth and respect of others.

All of these masks hide the real villain: separation from the root, or disconnectedness. When you lose connection, you lose sight of the true self. When you lose connection, the invisible mirror is clouded over with doubt and ignorance. When you lose connection, you leave nothing behind but rotten fruit for the coming generation.

But it need not be so. When you are connected to the generations before you, when you are grounded in the present moment, when you are *plugged in* to your life's purpose, all of a sudden you become aware of this web of connection. From that moment on, you never feel isolated, you never feel alone.

Invisible Hunger

Within each of us there is a fundamental hunger for connectedness. We feel incomplete without a bridge to good friends, partners and spouses. But in a world dominated by the spirit of blindness, how can we choose these relationships wisely? How shall we satisfy the invisible hunger for connection and still have security? In a healthy relationship, the people around you will lift you up and you will lift them up, too. A good friend will act in the highest form of humanness: with respect, compassion, kindness and love. But there are others who set aside their humanness and give in to more brutish or animalistic tendencies. These people may be powerful and may even be superficially beautiful, but their lack of humanity is reflected in their behaviour. If you get too close to a tiger, it may bite you. You can't blame the tiger, because it was your choice to get into that position, and it was the tiger's nature to behave in that way. If someone exists in your life that you know can react impulsively, it is important to keep this in mind, because there is a good chance that they may act in a way that is incongruent to your path. Instead of letting it affect you or influence you too greatly, take a moment to remember your path and review their general character, and then you can choose how you would like to proceed in your relationship with them.

Similarly, you have the choice of which people to become close to. The Way of True-Right-Correct is a powerful tool for choosing relationships. Look within yourself and open the invisible eye to view your prospective friends. True friendship is based on a mutual kinship rooted in principle and a shared vision of travelling together along the mindful pathway leading to the highest form of humanness.

Such companionship is a bond not to be severed by hardship and difficult challenges in life. True friendship is more than shallow talk and words; it is deeply rooted, and demonstrated through the actions of loyalty, trust, togetherness, honour and mutual respect. True friendship satisfies the invisible hunger within. True friendship is a food. Sometimes sweet, sometimes sour – but it is always savoured with loyalty. When the friendship is sweetened by the joys of life, you relish it. When the friendship is soured by the pains of life, you do not spit it out. You take the smooth and the rough both, because true friendship is togetherness, no matter what happens. With true friendship, you are never alone. That is the way to success. That is the moral principle of friendship and of any relationship that we enter by choice.

True Relationships with Complete Trust

There is no true relationship without complete trust. Relationship without trust is a dawn with no sun, a fire with no warmth. How unfortunate it is when people feel they cannot trust one another. By withholding trust, they believe they are shielding themselves from harm. But the invisible hunger for connectedness can never be satisfied by withholding trust. Those who withhold trust are harming themselves within. They are feeding on their own self-doubt; they are nourishing themselves on their own emptiness. They are starving to death, by not learning how to trust other people. They go nowhere and their efforts end in failure.

I have been in many situations where I could easily have lost trust in people. You probably have, too. But if there is one thing I'm grateful for in this life, it is that I didn't get stuck in a place of distrust and bitterness. It doesn't mean that you don't observe people carefully and use your best judgment on whether someone is reliable. But the True-Right-Correct Method has been a reliable guide for me. And in the end, I truly believe that to live without trust is to lose touch with your humanity – and even your heart.

Those who spend their time learning to walk through life in a state of mistrust should instead spend that time learning how to place trust correctly in other people. Most of us know someone who has – or have ourselves – been hurt by a relationship. Some people decide that they will no longer have trust in people, though this is a road that leads to isolation. Others, on the other hand, continue to blindly and deeply place trust, and this often also leads to a recurring cycle of isolation. Others still find that placing trust *correctly* in others leads to connectedness.

How do they do this? They understand that deep trust is earned a little bit at a time, over the course of time. Consistency is the glue that bonds trust in a relationship. Inconsistency has the power to deteriorate or even shatter that bond, which may have taken many years to reach such strength. They do not cut off their willingness to trust, nor do they give deep trust away blindly.

One must use the pure "open" (spiritual) eye to place complete trust correctly in others. Trust does not follow the shrill *Doe Chi* voices of greed and selfishness or the shallow fickleness of superficial change. Trust follows the deep, still voice of enduring principle along the mindful pathway.

When you use the pure "open" eye to place trust correctly, your confidence in your judgment and your trust in yourself will grow and mature. If a colleague is accused of committing an error that, in fact, you have committed, you will follow that voice of enduring principle to choose your response. Using the correct form of trust leads to success in life. This complete trust is the way of honour.

A Pathway of Trust and Faith

For me, having faith in something greater and deeper than myself is vitally important. This isn't a perspective that I would force on anyone, but when people ask me how I face difficult circumstances, I have to say that I could not survive if I did not have faith.

All religion and spiritual belief systems are grounded in both trust and faith. If that is something that resonates for you, consider these principles of the Living Meditation pathway:

- The pathway of trust and faith was here long before you were born and will remain long after you die. Choosing this pathway is a key choice for success in life.

- A life without trust and faith may be rich in visible things but poor in invisible (spiritual) things.

- A life with trust and faith may be rich in both kinds of wealth: visible things in sufficiency, invisible (spiritual) things in abundance – balance, harmony, pure relationships, true friendships, peace and joy.

- Do we not teach our children up as well as down, in as well as out, night as well as day? So why do we so rarely teach them the correct way to trust others, rather than just how to be constantly in a state of self-defence?

- Walls will tumble, swords will rust and armies will fade away. The only secure way to protect our children forever is to teach them to be their own guard through pure (correct) trust and correct perspective.

- To know how to trust correctly is to learn to see through the pure "open" (spiritual) eye.

The Good Gardener

Knowing your true self is a choice. Like a gardener, you can clear away the weeds of doubt and insecurity before they choke off the growth of the tender plants. You can cultivate the soil of honour. You can channel the waters of respect. You can nourish plants with faith and hope, looking toward the harvest. You can preserve the connection to the root. You can grow good seeds to pass on to your children and the coming generations. You can see the true self clearly in your invisible mirror. You can choose the mindful pathway.

If, for a time, you have strayed from the main path, you can return to the high ground. If, for a time, you have wandered onto the wrong pathway, you can repair the invisible harm and reclaim the task of cultivating good seeds for the coming generations. If, for a time, you have allowed material things to possess you, rather than you possessing them for the good of others, you can change your reality. You can discard the masks and silence the voice of *Doe Chi*. You can glow with the light of honour and shine with the light of humanness in its highest form.

But this is not something to put off until tomorrow. As the good gardener knows, the growing season is short. The harvest is near. When I was a child, my father taught me that every day lost is two days spent – one wasted on the wrong path, another catching up on the right path. Happily, though, the way of mindfulness pays a thousand-fold, for the good seeds spread without end, season after season, until destiny brings you and the coming generations to the top of the mountain, to the highest form of humanness.

"To know how to trust correctly is to learn to see through the pure "open" (spiritual) eye."

KEY SIX: YOUR REALITY FOR THE BETTER

We all have the ability to change our realities for better or for worse.

When we let outside factors influence our inner selves, our realities are always emotionally turbulent. Negative situations feel imprisoning and we lose sight of ourselves and our goals. When we let our inner world determine our outer reality instead, we can cultivate a sense of deep peace and strength that carries us through every situation. We become empowered. We can take on challenges and handle times of tension and discomfort with a new sense of ease, knowing that they are temporary. We are able to hold a clear vision for greater things on the horizon.

My father once told me a story about living in the mountains of Korea, during his years as a student of meditation. In the first few years, he would sometimes find himself beginning to get restless. Then his master would tell him, "When you are living in this cave you may think you are locked in, but remember there was a time when you were in your mother's womb and you did not feel locked in. This is because you had inner peace, and you were not influenced by your surroundings. The same can be true of any situation."

At times, you may find yourself in a negative situation or period in your life and feel imprisoned by your current reality, which can lead down a path to isolation, sadness, anger and disconnectedness.

But just as quickly as you can flip a switch and turn a dark room bright, you can also change your reality.

So, how do you make this happen?

The ability to change your reality lies inside of you. What often trips people up is the act of looking outward to find out who we are, only to encounter a maze of tangled paths that lead in so many directions. Magazines, social media, other people's opinions – we can end up encountering so many detours that take us not very far from where we started and leave us feeling overwhelmed and anxious.

This is why the great sages have always taught that we should look inward for the correct path to be revealed.

We tend to think of changing over time, in an extended process, but each moment is new and stands on its own. We have to be present in the moment and remind ourselves, "I'm changing my reality right now, in this moment," and move forward.

When you know yourself, you become accountable. When you become accountable, you understand that you are in charge of your destiny, your life. You have the power to choose what you do from this moment forward. And, as you practise the process of changing your reality in a single moment, you learn to let go of ideas, concepts and paradigms that do not enhance your life and that create imbalances. You are able to let them go and change them for ones that lead you down a good and mindful path.

This path of change is not an easy one to follow at first. You will encounter countless challenges that will make you want to veer away in the desire for a more comfortable situation, but unless you take on these challenges you will not grow. Each obstacle along your path presents an opportunity to gain more wisdom and inner peace.

Once you achieve inner peace, it does not matter where you are, because your surroundings will not affect you. You will feel secure and comfortable no matter the situation. With inner peace you have the ability and awareness to change your own reality for the better and, in turn, positively affect the reality of those around you.

For my father, learning that he could change his reality involved a very literal and specific challenge: climbing a mountain path filled with obstacles.

There was silence in the valley, interrupted only by the occasional cooing of a mourning dove. Master Borion and my father were walking silently along the path that led through a grove of trees.

Finally, Master Borion spoke. "Body and mind off balance."

Startled, my father replied, "It is true that I have a queasy feeling in my stomach, but how did you know? I am walking normally. I am talking normally."

"I know through wisdom," said his teacher. "Wisdom sees hidden things in the eyes, in the face."

"I do not want to be sick," replied my father.

"Look at that small tree," said Master Borion. "What do you see?"

"Many leaves," said my father.

"Many leaves, yes. But look carefully at the colours. A few of the leaves are a different shade – much browner. These leaves are sick, ready to drop. The others are healthy. Life is not much different than that. Some stay connected, some don't."

"To be truthful," responded my father, "I haven't felt well since we ate that soup yesterday. Really, I'm feeling very sick. How can I be healed?"

"Change your reality," replied Master Borion.

"My reality?"

"This sickness is your reality. You can change your reality. That is always your choice."

"How do I do that?"

At that, Master Borion reached into the folds of his robe and removed a small sprig of green. "You should gather this herb and use it," he said. "That way you will learn knowledge and begin to earn wisdom."

"Where do I find this herb?" asked my father.

His teacher turned and looked off into the distance toward the white peak on the horizon. "Up there, on the summit of the mountain."

"You mean you want me to go up there and find it?"

"Do you want to be well again?" asked Master Borion.

"Yes."

"Then learn to change your reality."

"But, Master, there is a raging river between here and that mountain."

"Yes," said Master Borion calmly.

"And, Master, the summit is surrounded by treacherous cliffs."

"Yes," said Master Borion in a relaxed voice.

"And, Master, I don't know how to climb those cliffs."

"Yes," replied Master Borion serenely.

"And, Master, there are dangerous animals that live on the mountain."

"Yes," said Master Borion. "Take this herb and match it exactly. Life challenges us to choose good or bad. You hold the choice. When you learn to change your reality for the good, you have the opportunity to earn wisdom."

My father swallowed hard and felt the ache in the pit of his stomach.

"I will go," he said, and bowed in reverence.

The next day, toward evening, Master Borion heard a knock on the door of his cottage. It was my father, bent over with exhaustion and sickness, his clothing torn, his arms and hands bruised and scratched. But he beamed with satisfaction as he pulled a thatch of greenery from his shirt. "I have found it, Master," he said, "the herb."

Master Borion took a sample of it in his left hand and the original in his right hand. He brought them close together until they touched. "It is correct," he said. "They match. Now go and change your reality."

Confused, my father asked, "But how shall I use this herb? Do I just eat it?"

"Make tea," said his teacher.

"But I don't know how."

"That is your reality," replied Master Borion. "Change your—"

"Reality," interrupted my father.

Master Borion smiled and turned away. As he closed the door, he said, "First learn, then earn. To change your reality, start from the beginning. Remember, you are not a brown leaf on the tree. Stay connected."

Bewildered, my father walked down the pathway to his shelter, where he fumbled first with one utensil and then with another. Finally, he succeeded in crushing the herbs and placing them in boiling water to steep. Then he poured a cup of tea and sipped it slowly.

Before long, he could feel fingers of warmth and power moving through his body. Soon he felt complete relief. Running back to the cottage, he once more knocked on the door.

Master Borion appeared. "Yes?"

"Thank you, Master. I am greatly relieved."

"Do not thank me," said Master Borion. "Thank yourself. Now you know in this situation how to change your reality."

"How did this sickness happen?" asked my father. "I'm young and healthy – I've never been sick until now. Why didn't you get sick from the soup?"

"All of your life you have been building Wae Gong*, external*

strength," said Master Borion. "Never Nae Gong, *inner strength."*

"I did not know about inner strength, Master."

"Very few know about inner strength," replied his teacher gravely. "It is the key to great internal balance and power. With it, you can overcome physical sickness. When you learn this, you will be able to help many others to be stronger. That is earning."

My father fell silent at these words.

"With this inner strength, you and the mountain are truly one," Master Borion continued.

My father turned his eyes again toward the summit from which he had just returned.

"First learn, then earn," said his teacher. "Through the herb you can earn relief for the moment. Through the journey, you can earn the secret of life forever."

"It is good," said my father, but his eyes said something else.

"You have a question," observed Master Borion.

"Yes," replied my father, gathering his courage. "I was sick. I was helpless. Why didn't you help me more with the climb and with the tea?"

Master Borion put his arm around my father's shoulders. "When the young eagle first flies, it flies alone. The parents are nearby, not too close and not too far away. I was behind you all the way. You can gain knowledge from others, but wisdom you must gain by yourself. Wisdom is greater than knowledge. Knowledge can divide; wisdom connects. I will not always be with you. Therefore, the time for you to start gaining wisdom is now."

My father bowed his head reverently. "Master, this inner strength is deep."

"The secrets of inner strength are the wings of wisdom," said Master Borion. "With inner strength you speed the journey toward the highest form of humanness."

"Why have you not taught me inner strength before?" asked my father.

"You were not ready yet," responded his teacher. "But it is now time to teach you the ways that will connect you, that will make you one with the mountain. You will learn to work with nature – with wind, fire and water – the source of great inner strength. Once you have learned how to connect in this way, you can use inner strength to help heal many others and help them, in turn, to gain inner strength. First you learn, then you earn. To earn through helping others is the key to happiness."

"And I will be able to help others restore themselves of illness, Master?"

"Yes," confirmed Master Borion. "Once you have learned inner strength, you will begin to earn the good seed to pass on to your children and many others, including coming generations. The good seed is balance, harmony, peace, joy and great external and internal strength."

"When do we begin?" asked my father.

"With the next lesson."

A Choice in Every Moment

Over many generations, Living Meditation wisdom has taught that life challenges us to choose good or bad. In every moment, we have a choice. Do I want to drink this tea now? Shall I put on a sweater now? Will I stand and stretch now? Good or bad is within each of us. We can choose to follow one path or the other. If we follow the blind pathway, we move in the direction of imbalance, selfishness, shallowness of character, isolation and corruption. If we follow the mindful pathway, we move in the direction of harmony, balance, compassion, togetherness and integrity.

In Western culture, when we talk about good and bad, it seems a very binary notion. The philosophy I was raised with and that lies at the heart of Living Meditation sees it a little differently. The best way to describe it is with a visual someone shared with me not long ago.

You are probably familiar with the yin and yang symbol (see page 45). In Chinese philosophy, Tao is the absolute principle underlying the universe, combining within itself the principles of yin and yang and signifying the way or code of behaviour that is in harmony with the natural order. In this symbol, the dark circle and the dark swirl are yin, which is associated with femininity, quiet, contraction and night-time. The light circle and the light swirl are yang, which is associated with brightness, masculinity, expansion and daytime. They are always together, one within the other, always transforming and moving together, always working toward balance. The bad is in the good, the good is in the bad. Together, this is life.

Movement is essential: to life, to change. We can find balance within ourselves through eating properly, by taking supplements to nourish our bodies, by meditating and calming our minds and bodies, but also through movement. Any kind of movement is good, whether it is weightlifting or Pilates, martial arts, yoga or running. All of these practices help us become aware of our own condition and find that sense of balance and harmony by removing stagnation and promoting proper flow of vital energy (or chi).

Many people do not clearly see that life offers them this grand choice of good or bad. Instead, they see themselves as victims of their surroundings and circumstances. They are weighed down by thoughts such as:

If I had been born in a different city, things would be better for me.

I can trace all of my misfortune directly to my upbringing.

My life would be easier if people didn't keep getting in my way.

I really have no direction in life.

They see themselves defined by their own reality, rather than holding the power to define their own reality.

Reality is Growth

Reality is what we see and believe concerning our surroundings and ourselves. Many people see reality as something fixed, something that holds them back. For them, reality is a prison. They stare each day at the four walls of their reality and feel locked in. They see bars on the doors and windows. They see nothing but restraints to their progress, with no way to escape.

But there is another way to look at reality. You can look at your reality as something that you can change. You can see genuine opportunity at every turn. You can see reality not as a prison, but as an environment that is dynamic, challenging and full of choices. You can see reality as a condition of growth and improvement. By making correct choices in this kind of dynamic reality, you move toward humanness at its root centre, the highest form of humanness.

This is what I think of when I recall my father's story about the prison and the womb. I don't believe that a child in its mother's womb is isolated or alone. To the contrary, this is the point of highest, deepest connection in our lives. To your mother, to the world around you – in the womb you are part of the never-ending thread of connection.

On the other hand, if we feel caged in by our reality and allow it to control us, we do not grow spiritually but remain at a base level of existence, having neither hope for a better future nor the wisdom to create it. We lose sight of our true self and must hide behind the masks of insecurity, envy and blame. Since we have lost sight of our own potential, we cover our insecurity by blaming our misfortunes and shortcomings on other people or on circumstances or both. We boast of our personal strength while tearing others down. We spend our time in gossip and accusation. We spend our energy making up excuses, rather than using this same energy to change our reality for the better. The problem is: many of us don't know how to change our reality.

How to Change Your Reality

There are three steps for changing your reality:

1. Open your invisible eye and see your true self having the potential of unlimited progress. With one glance of your invisible eye, prison walls dissolve and restraints disappear. Excuses pass away like dry leaves in a fire, like dust in the wind, like foam on the ocean waves. You see yourself with choices for good and for bad, and you choose the good, the mindful pathway.
2. Follow the Way of True-Right-Correct. By choosing to improve yourself and gain a greater perspective – no matter what your circumstances – you lift yourself up in correct ways to serve others. Through continual movement (learning and earning), you gain in understanding and wisdom. You move forward like the deep waters of a great river flowing to the ocean. You begin to grow the invisible seeds to pass on to your family and to your community as a legacy of love and connectedness.
3. Go with nature as the source of great energy. Connect with this natural flow of energy through movement and mindfulness. Changing your reality requires not only external strength but great internal strength. The principles of Living Meditation have been passed down for centuries as the means to connect with natural energy – the power of vitality in life, chi, the Tao, the universe. It is this connection that promotes health and pours extraordinary healing influences over the participant.

These three steps are tools of destiny. By using them, you accelerate your progress along the correct pathway and rise on the wings of wisdom. Through wisdom you earn your way on the journey of life. Earning your way means serving others as you serve yourself. By bringing natural energy into your mind and body, you gain tremendous power to do good. By giving of your true self, you find your true self.

Change Your Perspective, Change Your Life

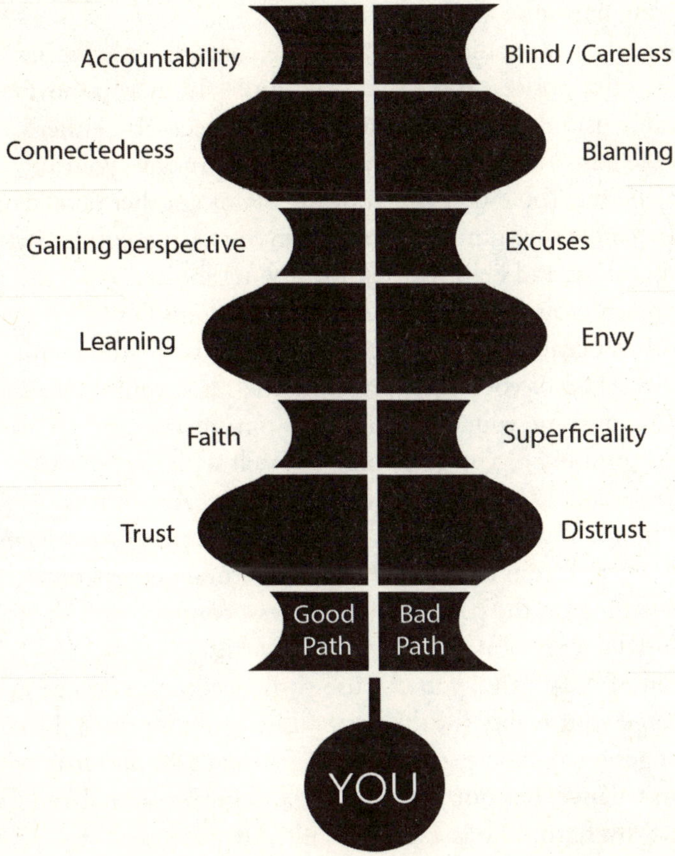

By changing your perspective, you can change your life. Change your perspective by being aware of what you see in the invisible mirror – a clear perspective of your choices in life.

Place yourself in the circle in the illustration (above). This is your present position, your "reality".

Life challenges us to choose good or bad. By following the blind path of carelessness, you move toward confinement and weakness, eventually becoming less than human. By following the mindful pathway, you move toward liberation and vitality, eventually reaching the highest form of humanness and achieving harmony and happiness.

Based on your choices, you associate yourself with a series of pairs of opposites. You either drift aimlessly, or you move resolutely using the Way of True-Right-Correct. You either live a life based on excuses, or you learn to improve your life for the better. You either live your life blaming other people or circumstances for your misfortunes, or you earn goodness by healing others and helping them. It is your choice.

Similarly, you can be weighed down in groundless pessimism because of self-doubt or you can rise joyfully with an active sense of your emerging potential. It is your choice. You can consume your time with false optimism based on wishful thinking or you can guide yourself with hope and faith based on a certain vision of your future. Again, it is your choice. You can continue in the drunkenness of *Doe Chi* (disconnected from the source of great natural energy) or, by remaining on the path of mindfulness, connect with the unlimited energy of nature and the universe.

In all of these cases, you can use your freedom of choice to change your reality for the better. Life is not a prison. Life challenges us to choose good or bad, giving us an opportunity to gain balance, harmony, peace, joy, and great external and internal strength. Life is a time to cultivate good seeds to pass on to the coming generations as a legacy worth remembering forever.

Everyday Choices

Every single day, we face so many choices. We choose and we go with the flow. Things are always flowing, always balancing. Life itself is never stagnant.

The process might not always be simple – I won't tell you that life is simple, or easy, all the time – but the moment of decision is as simple as flipping a switch.

I say this to myself, and I say it to my sons all the time. "You have two choices. What do you wish to choose?" Sometimes when you make matters that simple, reducing it to black and white like the yin and yang symbol, it helps you to see things a little more clearly.

Even at the age of seven, this idea of choices resonates strongly for my older son Vince. We often have conversations that sound something like this:

"How do you want this afternoon to go? You can keep fighting against doing your homework and we can spend the afternoon arguing about it, when all day I've been waiting for this moment to see your beautiful face. Or are you going to make the choice you usually do, and just get your homework done so we can do something fun?"

I can see his face transform as he considers it. I can see him thinking, *You're right. This is totally in my hands right now.*

Such a thought is empowering, even liberating, whether you are seven, seventeen or seventy!

Here are some of the questions we all face in our daily lives, framed in black and white terms.

Why would you seek to blame others when you can take accountability for how your reality unfolds?

Why would you "imprison" yourself in a situation when you have the power to set yourself free, change your perspective and change your reality? And, in turn, the reality of your family and those around you that your choices affect?

Why would you suffer from insecurity and self-doubt when you can make a choice to gain perspective, make correct decisions and be grateful for the positives you have in your life?

Why would you succumb to unfounded pessimism, on the one hand, or shallow optimism, on the other, when you can move forward with hope based on an enlightened vision of your future?

Why would you tolerate an unhealthy condition when you can live a life of health and wellness?

Why would you grow stagnant when you can be continually moving (earning and learning)?

Why would you leave behind "rotten fruit" as a legacy when you can leave behind good seeds of harmony, balance, integrity, compassion, happiness and inner strength?

In short, why would you become anything less than your greatest potential? You have the choice.

So how do we do this in our daily life?

It only takes a few moments and can be done anywhere. When you find yourself in an imbalanced or stressful situation, take a breath. For me, I like to focus on the point right between my brows. Your eyes can be open or closed.

Become of aware of yourself and physically feel yourself become more grounded. Then you can make a choice if you want to respond or react. By taking this moment and becoming aware and accountable, you will be able to make a clear decision. By becoming clear inside yourself, you are then able to harmonize the situation or the person in front of you.

With this sixth key of Living Meditation, I hope you are starting to see how all of the eight keys build on each other. It's a little like learning one yoga pose, then another and then letting them flow together: the flow is greater than the sum of their parts.

If you are feeling that the idea of choice is daunting, I would encourage you to see it instead as an empowering and liberating idea. You are no longer constrained by circumstances or what other people think or say about you, by the events of your past or your expectations of your future. This life of yours is in your hands, even though it doesn't always feel that way. We all walk through circumstances that can be tough, even terrible at times. But by knowing our true selves, making correct daily choices, seeing our circumstances clearly, leaving a legacy of goodness and living with honour – these are the ways we can change our reality for the better.

"Life is a time to cultivate good seeds to pass on to the coming generations as a legacy worth remembering forever."

KEY SEVEN:
IT ONLY TAKES ONE MATCH TO LIGHT A THOUSAND

My father was my greatest mentor. He was my everything. He was a man of deep compassion, empathy, wisdom, and perspective. Above all else he taught me that the most important thing in life is to be a good person – and then everything will unfold as it should.

He was certainly strict: I was raised with a strong sense of tradition, duty and respect for my elders and for my lineage. Even so, he always allowed me to find my own path. Just before I decided to study Eastern Medicine and share our lineage's formulas with the world, my father asked me one simple question.

"Do you want to be special and achieve something in this life? To make this world better?"

Of course, I answered, "Yes."

"Then never be afraid to be different; and when everyone else is sleeping, you keep moving."

I have never stopped.

I lost my father when I was thirty-three years of age. He has never stopped teaching me, though. The lessons he taught me while he was physically here have reached me even deeper than they ever did while he was on this earth. I now have to stand on my own two feet, moving through experiences and obstacles, being very in tune and connected to myself and to the universe. By being this way, I am able to hear my father's voice in my mind, guiding me along my path.

A heavy mist was blanketing the countryside when my father opened his sleepy eyes and rose slowly from his bed before dawn. Too quickly the time for his lesson with Master Borion was approaching. His body still ached from the hours of intense training the evening before. Truly he felt like staying in bed. But he recalled his teacher's parting words: "The victory of the mindful path over the careless path is the victory of mind over matter." So my father hurried out the door and groped his way up the trail through the fog.

By the time he reached Master Borion's cottage, the first rays of dawn were beginning to clear the air.

Perhaps it will be a good day after all, thought my father as he knocked on the door.

Moments later Master Borion appeared. "Good morning, Master," my father said, bowing respectfully.

Master Borion spoke not a word, but looked around as if he did not see anyone at his doorstep.

"Good morning," repeated my father, putting on his broadest grin.

"I hear a voice," said Master Borion, reaching down to take up a handful of earth, "and I see footprints in the pathway, but there is nothing here but this clay."

"Here I am," objected my father, pointing at himself.

"Body here, maybe," said his teacher. "Mind not here."

My father lowered his head. "I was sore and tired from the practice yesterday. Sleep did not come easily because I was so uncomfortable."

"Did you want to come this morning?" asked Master Borion.

"Yes, of course."

But Master Borion frowned and raised a finger.

"Well, the pillow was tempting," admitted my father, "but I am truly happy to be here now."

"Feelings change constantly," replied his teacher. "Body sore, body rested; body tired, body fresh; body hungry, body full: many different feelings. If you go by how you feel in any given moment, you will lack focus and direction – like walking through the forest in a dense fog. But when you go by True-Right-Correct, you go by principle, and principle never changes. How do you feel now?"

"I am ready to learn more," declared my father.

Master Borion smiled. "Now your truth changes. Before, you did not want to practice your lesson. Now you do."

"Yes, Master," replied my father, following Master Borion into the cottage. "Now I am beginning to understand."

Master Borion placed his handful of clay into my father's hands, which he held in his own and squeezed gently. "Winning in life means winning yourself. Winning yourself means winning your mind and body. You will mould yourself like this clay. You will learn to make correct decisions no matter what you are feeling at the moment. That will give you strength and peace. Do you see this jar?"

My father fixed his eyes on a beautiful earthen jar placed on a small stand nearby.

"This jar has been passed down over many generations by wise teachers," said Master Borion. "One day soon it will be yours. It was prepared by skilled hands using just the right mixture of water and clay, just the right heat of the oven, just the right air in cooling. What is this jar used for?"

"To hold grains and fruits," answered my father.

"Yes," replied Master Borion. "You, too, will be a vessel like this, a living vessel for carrying the good seeds of compassion and wisdom for the coming generations. But you have much to learn before you can rise up with wisdom. Most importantly, you must learn that truth is a deception."

Shocked at these words, my father asked what his teacher meant.

"If you follow only the truth you feel at the moment," replied Master Borion, "you are on the downward path. Truth with feelings without using Correct is the wrong way. That is the way of Gan Sa: endless changing, endless flux. Tell me, is this not a deception?"

"Yes," agreed my father.

"But if you act on true and right by following what is correct, you are on the good pathway. Superficial Gan Sa truth is

based on constant change. Eternal truth is based on never-changing principle. That is wisdom."

"I understand," said my father. "My truth now makes me want to practice, because it is correct. It is the good way of mindfulness."

"That is right," confirmed Master Borion. "Mind over matter. Your spirit and mind are learning to control your body and your actions. If you go out and try to face tigers with laziness and lack of self-control, you will not survive. Do not forget why you are here. Life never ceases to challenge us to choose for better or for worse, for good or for bad. That is why you should train your mind and body. Go and practice now, and afterwards come to see me in the Am Ja."

For the next few hours, my father practiced the difficult exercises and movements of his training. Mind over matter, he kept thinking. Living vessel of wisdom, he kept saying over and over to himself. "Leave good seeds behind," he whispered. He felt the rhythm of his movements, and he felt harmony and peace. By the time he was through, his mouth was parched and dry, and his clothing was drenched with perspiration. Then he went to the Am Ja as his teacher had instructed him.

Drained and thirsty, my father bowed before Master Borion. His eyes then caught sight of some items on the table: a bowl of water, a dish of roasted mountain vegetables and a portion of rice.

With a gesture, Master Borion directed my father to be seated. "Is it really true that you are thirsty?" he asked.

"Yes," replied my father.

"Then drink," said Master Borion. My father eagerly did so.

"Are you still thirsty?" asked his teacher.

"Not anymore."

"So your true feeling has changed?"

"It has," confirmed my father.

"Is it true you are hungry?" asked Master Borion.

My father's eyes returned to the food, and its delicious aroma tickled his nostrils.

Master Borion smiled. "Then eat," he said. Quickly my father overcame his shyness and ate until every morsel was gone.

"Are you hungry now?"

"No, master."

"No longer hungry," observed Master Borion. "So your truth has changed again. How do you feel now?" My father bowed in response and silently waited.

"In our daily life," continued Master Borion, "feelings change constantly. So our truth changes constantly. What is the name for that?"

"Gan Sa," answered my father.

"Yes," said Master Borion. "Truth from Gan Sa is always changing. This truth is like dry leaves in autumn – spiralling down and around, carried every which way by the shifting winds. Many times this superficial truth is without Correct. If

you act upon such truth, thinking it is right, when it is not correct, you are on the careless pathway. Your actions do not do the most good for the most people. Do you understand?"

"Yes," said my father, "I understand that Correct is based on principle, and principle never changes."

Master Borion put his arm around his student's shoulder. "Come, let us walk to the valley. Perhaps you can add more to your wisdom this day."

Living vessel of wisdom, thought my father to himself, and he smiled. Presently they came to a place where the trail divided itself into three pathways, all of them leading down into the valley. "Which path shall we take?" asked Master Borion.

"I would be pleased to have you choose," replied my father.

"Yesterday we took the path on the right," said Master Borion. "Today let us follow the one on the left. What do you see now?"

Thinking for a moment, my father then answered, "Master, I am beginning to see things more clearly. Gan Sa is always looking for change, variety, something different. That is often no good."

Master Borion replied, "Yes, Gan Sa is a dangerous addiction. Gan Sa is consumed with itself so much that it blocks the view of the Correct. Gan Sa is matter over mind. Wisdom is mind over matter. Wisdom is the mindful way of balance, compassion, peace and joy. Look down there at the valley. What do you see?"

My father saw that the fog was still lingering over the valley, and he kept silent.

"Up here in the mountain," continued Master Borion, "our choices are few. Down there in the valley the choices are many. That is the realm of Gan Sa, the realm of confusion and flux. That is why you need practice – mentally and physically. With practice you win. When you have light and faith, nothing breaks you. With light and faith you make correct decisions. You become light in your true self. If you are light, there is no darkness, no fear. Nothing can destroy you. How do you feel?"

My father replied, "Much stronger, Master."

"When you follow the mindful pathway," said Master Borion, "your light helps others. It is up to them to accept it and learn from it. When they learn, they too become light. Your sharing is your earning, the good seed. What light you pass on to others is the true earning. When you are light, others come to you. You are a living vessel of wisdom, a living vessel of light. Do you understand?"

"Yes, Master," my father replied, feeling a warmth in his heart.

Master Borion finished the lesson with these words: "Light intimidates the night. Light never intimidates those who seek to act with Correct, because that is the way to help others. One must follow the light to become light. Light dispels the fog of Gan Sa. Now, go on from here alone and practice to become light."

"Yes, Master," said my father, bowing. "I truly look forward to the next lesson … but what is the key to winning mind over matter?"

"One of the ways to win the battle of mind over matter and gain enduring inner strength is through Living Meditation," replied Master Borion. "Tomorrow I will begin to teach you a way to open up the inner eye and find the way of success."

Become a Living Vessel of Wisdom

In a far-off Asian country, there was once a King who drank special elixirs that kept him healthy, beautiful and young for a long time. The Royal Court – and *only* the Royal Court – could partake of those *Bibong* formulas (which translates to "secret formulas" in the Korean language). They were kept under lock and key by his expert formulators, handed down from one generation to the next in a lineage of herbologists over many centuries.

One day, the empire was abolished and the King surrendered his throne.

Sounds like the first page of a novel, doesn't it? And if I were the reader of that book, I would want to turn the page and find out… What happened to those fabulous elixirs and the formulators who made them?

But I don't have to turn the page. I know the rest of the story because the story is true. The royal line of that Asian country that partook of those secret formulas – it actually existed. And the lineage of herbologists who made them and kept them under lock and key – they also existed. How do I know? Because I am the last living descendant of that lineage, entrusted with guarding those formulations.

I was well groomed for this serious responsibility, and just like my ancestors, I didn't take it lightly. I studied Traditional Oriental Medicine, I received my doctorate degree and excelled in herbal medicine, and I was mentored by my father who taught me the secret, ancient science of *Bibong* herbal formulas.

But unlike my ancestors, who were dedicated to keeping these formulas and the science behind them under lock and key, I had something different in mind.

Something that seemed outrageous, even impossible. I wanted to share them with the world.

But who was I to change a millennium-old tradition steeped in unchangeable culture? Not only was I the first woman to be entrusted with such a precious heritage, I was the first Asian-American woman to be given this royal honour. You can only imagine how my modern "female" intention of sharing this history of priceless knowledge would go over in my culture.

Impossible.

When I shared my intention with my father, he encouraged me, in that very conversation I mentioned at the beginning of this chapter.

"Jenelle, if you want to be special and accomplish the impossible, you must never be afraid to be different. But remember this," he said, "it only takes one match to light a thousand."

I grew up with an understanding that if you totally put your mind and heart into something, it will flourish. Whether it is doing calligraphy, or dancing, or singing, you'll achieve everything that you wish to achieve.

Deep in my heart and soul I felt that I had a limited time with my father and not one minute could be wasted, so I have always felt this need to race time. I set my mind and committed myself to learning from him every waking moment that I had. In order to be the guardian of the secret formulas I have had to sacrifice a lot and I have had to grow up quickly. I always followed my heart even when my mind tried to persuade my heart that I should take some time to relax, go out with my friends, take a break – but I knew that this was not what was going to help me to achieve my wish of learning all that I possibly could.

And then it happened: my worst nightmare. One evening after a beautiful day, just like the flip of a switch, my father passed for no known reason at all. I was with him the moment that he passed. He was as healthy as anyone, even as someone my own age. Clearly, he had completed his mission in this life and it was his time to return to heaven. This was one of the most lucid moments when I knew that all of the sacrifices had been worthwhile. I am reminded of it every time I look at my two young boys.

When I am tired because I am only able to sleep for three hours and deadlines on projects are flying by and my kids are yearning for my attention, I think of all of the opportunities that I have been given in my life. I look at my boys and I know that each of these sacrifices lead to a life of meaning and purpose that will extend to them. This is the power of a mother, a woman: strength and flexibility. These secrets have a humble power, which is the strongest kind. It is a power that runs deep.

Before my father passed away, he taught me key lessons that would help me to be the "match that lights a thousand".

The most important lesson was this: Set your mind and your intention, and plug in to the Tao.

How do I follow the Tao? What is the Tao?

The Tao is simply the universe. In my life I believe that all answers are within me and around me and if I surrender myself to the Tao, have complete faith in the universe, and look inside myself, then I will always find the answer. The answers and feelings will arise deep from within myself, from my intuition that is connected to the Tao – the universe. It is a universe filled with consciousness that will help guide me on my authentic, correct path.

The principles of the universe are never changing. They're never based on opinion. These never-changing principles are what we call wisdom.

So how do I apply this to my reality?

I'll describe to you a scene that I'm sure you will find familiar. We've all been there:

I'm ready to enter a boardroom filled with minds that already have an agenda. My mission is to open those "set-in-stone" minds to a new, expanded idea. I'm not only going to be the only woman in the room; I'm going to be the only Asian-American woman in the room. I'm younger than they are – and tinier too! Many of my ideas may feel unfamiliar, even uncomfortable to them, and I already know that this could result in resistance.

Those who came before me in my lineage who were the guardians of these secret formulas were men. They were 100 percent Asian and mature in years. But when I became the guardian of these secrets, I was a woman, an Asian-American, and I was young. However, none of these things stood in my way. When I step into a boardroom full of "powerful men", I have to remind myself not to overwhelm THEM.

This doesn't mean I disregard these things, these people. I always listen, but I don't always let it influence me – especially if it feels in resistance to my Tao, my path. I overwhelm them, not like a stiff board that is hard, taut and inflexible, but like bamboo – strong but flexible so as not to break … with knowledge, experience and wisdom that softly moves with the rhythm of the Tao, the universe.

So, before I enter an important meeting or speak in front of thousands, I plug in to the universe – to the Tao – and I hear my ancestors. Not with my ears, but with my heart; not with my physical eyes but with my invisible eye.

I plug in to the Tao, and I am never alone.

I begin to feel the consciousness of the universe enter my heart, strengthening my resolve, readying me to "start my impossible". I focus on the minds in the boardroom, imagining them yearning to expand just as much as I want to. I envision success.

I love asking myself questions, and I do it constantly. For me, it is a practice we all can turn to in order to purify ourselves on a daily basis. To measure your capacity for learning and imparting wisdom, you might ask yourself questions such as these:

To what extent are you a mender of differences, a peacemaker?
To what extent do people come to you for advice?

To what extent do you learn from your mistakes and experiences?

To what extent do your daily actions positively affect your family and your community?

To what extent is your focus on the "invisible" (cultivating the good seeds for the coming generations) rather than solely on the "visible" (tangible things that will not long endure)?

To what extent do you make it a priority to be "right" all the time, to "make your point" at all costs?

To what extent do you pour your cup before it is full (impart advice before you have learned wisdom through experience and effort)?

To what extent do you place higher value on knowledge than on wisdom (on learning facts rather than patterns that lead to doing the most good for the most people)?

It is always your choice whether to make correct and mindful or careless or self-indulgent decisions in this world. There are people who are never satisfied. They're always looking for something new, whether it's relationships or a job or a home. There's nothing wrong with having new things in your life, but there's a danger when you are not settled and not grounded, when you're constantly looking for new things.

Another key lesson my father taught me was to cultivate gratitude. It has become my spark, the spark that lights my match. Like everyone, I have times when the world feels heavy. It's at those times that the ability to expand my perspective into gratitude can pull me out of any moment that feels heavy or stressful. I realize that I'm grateful for my life. I'm grateful for my family. I'm grateful to have had the time with my father that I did, even though it was condensed more than I wanted or expected. I believe with unwavering certainty that it's not necessarily the sharing, educating and coaching that have afforded me the opportunities that I have in my life. Rather, it's the deep sense of gratitude I feel for being entrusted with this "impossible" pursuit.

For me, this is the heart of becoming a vessel of wisdom. It is an understanding that each one of us is connected to the people who are around us now, the ones that came before us, and the ones that will follow us. You know that my lineage is important to me, but it doesn't consist of my family alone. The beautiful thing is that while the heritage of the *Bibong* formulas has been handed down through generations in my family, there was a time where that was not so.

My father's teacher, Master Borion, was not my father's father. The good seeds that we leave behind, the wisdom that came before us and that moves on from us – these are not only for our own families, but for the world.

We have just come through a time in history when all of us could easily have felt entirely isolated. During the pandemic, many of us were in dark places, struggling with death and grief and solitude. But to have a glimpse of this notion that you are connected to the universe around you, the people who came before you and the ones who will come after, this brings me so much peace. You don't have to have a lineage. You don't have to have formulas. You don't even have to have a particular philosophy. It is enough to know that you are eternally connected, and you are never truly alone.

I am fulfilling the legacy of my lineage. To start my impossible and light my match, I DO have to work very hard while others sleep, and I am never afraid to be different. I fly on red-eyes all over the world to oversee, to speak and to educate. I stay up late and study. I am researching and developing new products all the time. And when I'm home, I tuck my boys in bed and tell them stories of healing from these centuries-old formulas, and their eyes go wide and they listen with eagerness. And just like my mentor – my father – told me, I tell them, "You too can start your impossible. It only takes one match to light a thousand."

One Match to Light a Thousand

Normally when I discuss or think of this principle, it is filled with positivity based on the understanding that it only takes one positive action, one person or one thought to ignite a thousand more. However, there is more to it than that.

Ultimately, just as there is night and day, loud and soft, masculine and feminine, yin and yang, there is always positive and negative. This means that just as this principle applies to the positive, it can also apply to the negative, meaning one negative action, person or thought can ignite a thousand more.

So, if we know the impact that even just one of our thoughts has, then we can be that much more aware of the fact that **each one of us holds the power** and has the choice in any and every situation to make our lives and the lives of those around us better or not. No moment is unimportant. You have the power to light the next match, there are always options to choose from, and each will have a ripple effect with a different outcome. Which match will you light?

"One positive action,
one person or one thought to
ignite a thousand more."

KEY EIGHT: BE LIKE BAMBOO

One of my favourite principles of Living Meditation to apply to daily life is *be like bamboo*.

So often in life it is easy to feel that being strong means being tough and rigid, but we have to remember that just like a stiff board, if we are too hard, too inflexible – when we are hit too many times or at a certain point – we can break.

Bamboo, on the other hand, is rooted deep and it is flexible. Even when a storm hits and strong winds push the bamboo to the ground, once the winds pass the bamboo bounces right back up.

Naturally, there are times to be hard and there are times to be flexible. This is the balance of life.

Therefore, instead of always being like a board that is hard, taut and inflexible, be like bamboo: strong but flexible so as not to break, with knowledge, experience and wisdom that softly moves with the rhythm of the Tao – the way of the universe.

It is so important to be fluid even in tough situations because through this fluidity we are able to move with the flow of nature while still being deeply rooted. This in turn allows us to live with greater awareness, connection and perspective, which will ultimately help us to create good habits and will bring us more happiness and peace in our everyday lives.

One of the main principles of Living Meditation is that of balance. When I use the word "balance," you may think of work-life balance. I want you to take one more step, go a little deeper and realize that balance starts from within you and from how you view a situation – and thus how you respond to it. It is from this internal balance that we are able to bring all of the external elements in our lives into balance as well. What happens within us is always the root cause of our happiness or our despair, our health or our suffering.

A person of balance responds to the daily challenges of life in correct ways that increase harmony, peace, wellbeing, joy and strength – not only for themselves, but for the people around them. With the inner eye, the person of balance sees clearly the "invisible thread" connecting all people through the consequences of their actions. They act calmly, remaining in control at all times, following unchanging principles on their mindful pathway. On the other hand, those who overreact or underreact to life's challenges respond out of misunderstanding, fear or anger. They have lost control of their lives, leading to selfishness, envy, abusive behaviours and isolation. The person of balance leaves a legacy of the good seeds for their family and the coming generation.

Only by learning to win the victory over self and opening the inner eye can we hope to achieve balance, calmness and control over our direction in life.

"There are times to be hard and there are times to be flexible. This is the balance of life."

KEY EIGHT: BE LIKE BAMBOO

There was a different feeling in the air that morning as my father was walking through the forest toward Master Borion's Am Ja. For the longest while, he couldn't put his finger on it. Then it came to him: silence. No birds chirping. No insects buzzing. No wind blowing. Nothing but silence. It was an eerie feeling. It made him feel uneasy and insecure. What was going on? What did he not understand?

Then he heard a crack behind him, followed by a creaking noise and a loud swishing. My father turned around just in time to see a massive old dead tree crash to the ground in an explosion of dust and noise, not ten feet away from him. Shocked, he hurried on nervously until he reached the Am Ja.

As usual, my father bowed and greeted Master Borion when he opened the door. But his teacher said nothing.

"Good morning," my father repeated.

Silence.

My father went ahead with the morning chores, fighting back an uneasy feeling. Was it something he had done, or failed to do? All morning he took great care to do everything correctly and avoid making any mistakes. From time to time my father felt Master Borion's eyes on him, but when he turned to see, his teacher was always looking in the other direction.

When the hour came for their morning walk, they headed toward the higher elevation of the mountain. Not a word was spoken. Then, along a certain level stretch of pathway, completely without warning, Master Borion lunged toward my father from the side with a shriek, as if attacking him. So surprised was my father that he bolted sideways, lost his balance and tumbled awkwardly to the ground with a thud. Master Borion had not so much as touched him and here he was in the dirt, completely disoriented.

Master Borion looked on with raised eyebrows as my father sheepishly got back up on his feet and brushed the dust from his clothing.

"What do you see?" asked Master Borion, his first words of the day.

"I was not expecting your attack," my father said. "Guess I overreacted."

"Overreacting when you are not in control can be death," Master Borion replied, ominously. "The principle is balance, calmness, control – no matter what happens."

"From you I was not expecting that kind of action," was my father's uncertain reply.

"I will not always be with you," Master Borion said. "While I am still with you, learn to be your own guard. Stay in control. Look and watch with the inner eye. That way there will be no surprises."

"Always be prepared," my father added, somewhat proud of himself for the idea.

"Yes, that is correct," Master Borion confirmed. "Know your true self – your strengths and weaknesses. Respond correctly to all circumstances – not too much reaction, not too little. Just enough to bring the most good to the most people and the least hurt. With my attack, you could have dodged quickly, in an agile manner, without loss of control. That is safety. That is being your own guard. Why did you not have control?"

To this question my father could think of no reply.

"Were you afraid?" Master Borion asked.

"No."

"Were you angry?"

"No."

"Did you misunderstand?"

"Misunderstand what?" my father asked.

"Were you surprised?" Master Borion replied.

"Yes."

"That is misunderstanding," Master Borion responded. "You believed there would be no threat, no surprise and in this you were mistaken. You misunderstood the situation. When there is understanding, there is no surprise – no matter what happens. Build on your strengths; overcome your weaknesses – that is control, that is self-discipline. Where there is control and self-discipline, there is calmness and balance. That is the principle."

"How can I always be in control?" my father asked.

"Open up the inner eye," Master Borion replied. "See the invisible thread."

"The invisible thread?" my father asked, puzzled.

"All things are connected," his teacher replied. "See those aspen trees over there. How many do you see?"

My father looked around at the vast grove of trees. "Many, perhaps hundreds," he replied.

"One," Master Borion said.

"One?" my father responded, startled.

"The root is one. All of them are interconnected – the invisible thread of life. With the inner eye, you see things from beginning to end. You see the results of your actions before you act. That way there is always correct action – no overreaction. You are in control through the invisible thread. When you are in control through the invisible thread, there is no fear, no anger, no misunderstanding, just calm."

They walked along in silence for a few minutes. My father kept a close watch on Master Borion from the corner of his eye. Finally, he asked a question that was gnawing at him. "Master," he said, "were you not overreacting back there when you jumped at me?"

"Yes," his teacher admitted. "Now you know one of my secrets – to overreact with purpose while in control. What do you see?"

"I see that I have learned an important lesson about being my own guard and not overreacting without control. Thank you, Master," my father said, bowing. Master Borion nodded.

"But, Master," my father continued, "why did you not speak to me this morning?"

"You are starting to understand," Master Borion replied. "What was the result?"

"I was certainly on guard," my father said. "And I did not want to make mistakes."

His teacher smiled. "Have you ever walked through the forest when everything turned silent?" he asked.

My father swallowed hard. "Yes," he said.

"Who knows?" Master Borion remarked. "Maybe the forest was watching you. Or maybe the animals and the insects saw something that you failed to see. Watch and learn. Stay in control. That is the way of calmness."

"And I should be silent, too, sometimes?" my father asked.

Master Borion looked directly into my father's eyes. "Many times in life when you encounter an opponent," he said, "your silence and inaction may serve to cover your intentions and keep the enemy off balance. That is to your advantage. Do you see that?"

"Yes," my father confirmed. "But how do you know when to overreact and when to underreact?"

"That", his teacher said, "will take a few years to learn. Down in the valley there are many people who have lost control of their lives. Every day they overreact from anger or fear or misunderstanding. Much harm can come from that. You can teach them a better way."

"And do they sometimes underreact?" my father wanted to know.

"Yes, that too," Master Borion replied. "Many underreact by being silent when they should speak, or by closing themselves off when they should connect, or by storing up when they should share. Teach them a better way. Teach them the way of balance. That way they can pass on the good seeds of harmony, joy, togetherness and peace in their families."

They stopped to rest for a few minutes next to a broad mountain stream. "Balance is deep," Master Borion said. "Deep water is calm as it moves slowly with purpose toward the sea. But shallow water in the frantic spring runoff is noisy and overreacting. Similarly, the closed pool grows stagnant and lifeless. That is underreacting where there is no control. Stay balanced. Stay in control. Stay calm."

In the distance, a hawk was circling endlessly on a current of air. A chipmunk squeaked from the shadows and a warm midday breeze rustled through the leaves of the aspen trees – or tree. And my father was peaceful.

Responding to Life's Challenges

The person of balance responds correctly to life's challenges, neither overreacting nor underreacting, but doing that which does the most good and causes the least harm for all. The person who overreacts or underreacts out of fear, anger or misunderstanding has lost control and cannot see the "invisible thread" connecting all people and events through a chain of consequences to action. Only by following unchanging principle using the inner eye can we achieve lasting peace, harmony, calmness and success.

This is what overreacting might look like:

- A father returns home after a hard day's work and walks into the house to see his teenage son sitting in front of the TV. He immediately shouts at his son, "Why didn't you take out the trash? Why didn't you feed the dog? What's the matter with you? You're just plain lazy!" With that the father storms out of the room – just as his son is trying to tell him that he had already done his chores.

- A woman who enjoys morning hikes hears on the news about another woman who was hit by a car while out hiking. The woman then stops hiking altogether because of her fear of being hurt. She never goes hiking again.

- A mother and her daughter are cleaning the house. While dusting, the daughter accidentally knocks over and breaks a valuable lamp. The mother snaps at her daughter, "You're so clumsy! You'll never grow up!" She slaps her daughter, who runs crying from the room.

This is what underreacting might look like:

- A man ignores the maintenance guidelines for his car and finds that it eventually stops running altogether, leaving his family without transportation.

• A young person asks their parent to help with a serious matter. "That's your problem," says the parent. "Take care of it yourself."

• A young child is stranded after soccer practice and their parent has not arrived after 30 minutes. When the last adult is leaving the area he thinks, *Her parents are probably on their way*, and drives off.

Those who, from loss of control, overreact or underreact to life's challenges cannot see "the invisible thread" that connects events, people and the consequences of action. Only the inner eye, in a state of calm control, can see clearly the interconnecting web of causes and effects that shape the context of our lives, both now and into the future. If we could see in the present moment – before we acted – the far-reaching future impact of our planned deeds, wouldn't we be very careful to act correctly? If we could see ahead of time what our words and deeds would do to help or harm ourselves, help or harm our loved ones, help or harm our communities, wouldn't we weigh everything carefully in the balance of lasting values and do that which would bring the most harmony, peace and joy to all concerned?

People of Balance

Over the centuries, Living Meditation has taught the principle of balance as a key to success and wellbeing. Balance is a primary quality of those who have "won themselves", who have learned to be their own guard on the mindful pathway. Those with balance of mind and body see situations and relationships with the inner eye, and they see how all things are connected. Before they act, they see clearly the consequences of those actions as a chain of interconnected events. People of balance can make correct decisions that will result in the most good for the most people, and the least possible harm for all concerned. They are in control and thus neither overreact nor underreact by mistake. They are calm because they follow natural principle. Natural principle leads to peace and harmony.

By way of contrast, some of us are blind to the consequences of our actions. We are controlled by fear, anger or a mistaken view of circumstances (misunderstanding). We tend to overreact or underreact to events and people around us. Often our action (or lack of action) results in harm to ourselves and those around us (family, friends and community). This dangerous condition too often poisons relationships in families, businesses and even nations.

Here's an example of the principle of balance.

A teenager borrows the family car and manages to get involved in a minor traffic accident. He places an anxious phone call, and his father picks up. "Dad," the confession begins, "I've had an accident with the car."

The father's response will conclusively demonstrate whether he sees the invisible thread or not. It may be either:

A calm, concerned voice says, "Are you all right? Is anyone hurt? Don't worry about the car. What can I do to help?"

Or:

An excited, angry voice shouts, "What did I tell you! What sort of idiotic thing have you done now? Can't you do anything right?"

In the first example, the foundation is laid for a careful, systematic, controlled solution to the problem and a strengthening of the relationship. The message will reverberate for years:

"You are important to me – not the car, not even the circumstances. We can take care of the visible things later. Right now the invisible things are important: you and your wellbeing."

This message will be a lasting testament to the father's love for their child. These words will stretch out like an invisible thread forever into the future.

In the second example, the overreacting father is out of control. His anger blinds him to the horrible reality of what he is saying. The words he has just spoken will likely never stop echoing in the mind of his son. They will always reverberate as proof of what the young person must surely suspect: the father places more value on the visible things and less on what really counts: the invisible values of harmony, peace, joy and vitality of those he loves. Because he has no balance, the father cannot see the enduring thread of pain stretching into the future without end.

Here's another everyday example. A couple goes out to dinner at a local restaurant. As they are waiting in line, a stranger accidentally bumps into the woman. Now her partner has a choice. He can turn on the stranger and confront him for his carelessness or he can pass over the incident and refocus on the evening with his wife. What if his wife, being upset by the incident, insists that he do something? Does he attack the stranger and trigger a series of events that may indeed ruin their evening out? Or does he survey the situation, weigh the options and decide that the option resulting in the most good for himself and his wife, and the least harm to all concerned, will be to recognize the event as an accident and continue with the evening's relaxation?

Perhaps this man, by staying in control of the situation, and following the principle of balance, will come to an instant conclusion that overreacting will punish the offender but destroy the evening out. He will signal to his partner that the aggressive alternative is not worth it in comparison with the projected evening of peace, harmony and relaxation.

This process of assigning "worth" to the outcomes of different options is a skill of the balanced person. That which offers the greatest worth to all concerned, resulting in the least harm, is the correct reaction.

Most often, both overreacting and underreacting come from the same three root causes: misunderstanding (misreading people or circumstances), anger (masking deep insecurity and imbalance) and fear (hiding insecurity, selfishness, unreadiness). When people do nothing or too little because of misunderstanding, anger or fear, they place themselves and others at risk. They often end up being out of control. They give up peace and harmony and instead react to the demands of uncontrolled emotions.

The diagram below offers a visual interpretation of the interconnection between underreacting, overreacting and balance.

Chart of overracting / underreacting

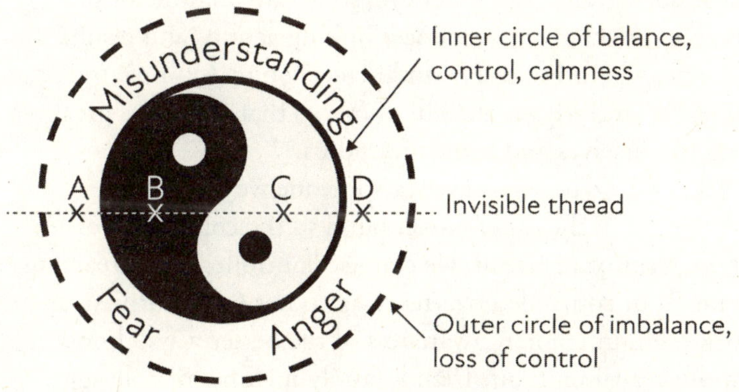

Key Locations

A. Uncontrolled underreacting
B. Controlled underreacting
C. Controlled Overreacting
D. Uncontrolled Overreacting

The inner circle of the chart (the yin and yang design) is the realm of balance, control and harmonious interaction of the active and receptive principles of life. The balanced person is at home within this circle. The outer circle represents an extreme degree of the yin and yang design, where fear, anger and misunderstanding prevail. When we dwell in this realm, we have lost control over our lives. We either underreact or overreact to life's challenges, becoming bound to emotion and the shifting pressures of the moment.

Running through these concentric circles is the "invisible thread" that connects all people and events. The person of balance can clearly see this thread and knows ahead of time what consequences will flow from different choices in life. Acting from calmness, they can make correct choices that will lead to increased harmony, peace, joy and togetherness for all concerned.

When we function in the outer circle, on the other hand, we cannot see with the inner eye, so we are unaware of the invisible thread of consequences linking actions and results. In this state, we unthinkingly underreact (point A) or overreact (point D), and trigger a chain of events that can cause great harm to ourselves and those around us.

What do we do when we see someone we care for functioning in the outer circle, blind to the consequences? As parent, mentor or friend, we can use controlled underreacting (point B) or controlled overreacting (point C) to surprise or shock them into a new awareness of the better way. Almost without realizing it, our friend, family member or colleague can be guided step by step back onto the mindful way where the invisible thread once more becomes visible. Once they learn to open their inner eye, the tyranny of anger, fear and misunderstanding crumbles, and peace, harmony, joy and togetherness can begin to emerge.

Calmness

Calmness is the opposite of uncontrolled overreacting and underreacting. Calmness prevails in the inner circle of the diagram above. There are two kinds of calmness: steady and immovable (at the very centre of the diagram) and borderline (at the fringes of the controlled space).

Steady and immovable calmness is like the root and trunk of a great tree. The root and trunk are unmoved and unaffected by the elements raging all around. The branches and leaves respond to the force of the winds and storms, but the root and lower trunk are steadfast. The person of calmness has a similar character. They remain in balance and control no matter what the circumstances. The solid foundation is built on root principle, which never changes. These people have learned to balance the active and receptive modes (yin and yang) so that correct decisions along the mindful pathway are made, leading to the highest form of humanness.

Borderline calmness is still controlled calmness, but this person is pushing hard from within to retain their balance in the face of the unrelenting challenges of daily life. There is a calm surface, but the inner core is still not without its tension. Such people must be on guard not to lose control of their lives and be drawn outside the yin and yang circle of balance and into the outer ring where misunderstanding, fear and anger prevail. Only the greatest focus on root principle and the greatest attention to the invisible thread can assure the borderline calm person a place in the centre of balance.

In this life we hold the choice between good and bad decisions. Each of us can decide to embrace one or the other. The way of calmness is the way of Living Meditation. It is the choice for harmony, balance, peace and joy. It is up to you to choose.

A Word about Perfection

Can anyone in this lifetime ever achieve complete balance, complete calmness, complete harmony? No; that possibility lies ahead of us, in a future sphere of existence. But in this life, in any given situation, we can learn to act so as to do the most good for (and the least harm to) the most people. For each of us, the proper reaction at the right time is the correct response.

We can learn to guide and channel things so that they work together to make our day the best it can be – for ourselves, for our families, for our workplace, for our community, and for the coming generations.

The classic overreacting or underreacting person says, "Nobody's perfect." The person of balance says, "We will make things the best they can be in this moment." The person of balance sees that every challenge can have its effect on those involved; therefore, the correct way of action is to do the most good for the most people. That is the invisible thread that holds us all together. That is the principle of balance.

In this book I hope that you will find some extraordinary solutions to many of life's most difficult challenges. All of these solutions come back to a few enduring principles of Living Meditation; principles that have existed for centuries.

The key to these basic principles is to view life as part of an eternal circle. In the morning we come new into this world ready to take on life's challenges. During the day we strive to pass the tests of life by making correct and wise decisions. In the evening we count the harvest and measure the legacy we leave behind when night comes upon us, through good seeds that will bear fruit for future generations.

"The key to these basic principles is to view life as part of an eternal circle."

ACKNOWLEDGEMENTS

ACKNOWLEDGEMENTS

To my parents: I have the highest love and gratitude for you. You are the reason.

To my siblings: we have been through so much together. I couldn't live without you.

To my uncles and extended family: I am so grateful to be on this path with you.

To Kathleen Gonzales, Sally Collings, Bill Gladstone, Anya, Laura and the entire team alongside me on this journey: you have helped clear a path for this book to become a reality. I could not appreciate you more.

To my husband and boys: I love you to infinity and beyond. My boys – it is my wish to pass these principles on to you, that you may use them as a guide throughout your lives, and continue to pass them on, leaving behind good seeds that bear good fruit for the coming generations.

One day maybe no one will remember my face, one day maybe no one will remember my name, but it is my ultimate wish to leave something positive behind for the benefit of all future generations. I am grateful to all who join me on this path.

ABOUT THE AUTHOR

Dr Jenelle Kim, DACM, L.Ac., is a Taoist longevity expert and ninth-generation doctor of Traditional Oriental Medicine, practitioner of qigong (moving meditation) and teacher of the eight keys of Living Meditation. A respected wellness authority, she has been featured in *Forbes*, *Allure*, *Meditation Magazine*, *TIME* and *Good Morning America*.

Dr Kim has been a devoted student of Eastern philosophy since childhood. Her writing and teachings draw from centuries-old principles passed down through her lineage – timeless wisdom that guides others to live with balance, clarity and purpose. As the daughter of an American mother and a Korean father, she bridges Eastern and Western thought through her unique 3M philosophy of Medicine, Movement and Mindset.

Once reserved for the ruling class, these teachings now reach audiences worldwide through Dr Kim's speaking engagements, her podcast The Experts and her platform, jenellekim.com.

In addition to her work as an author and speaker, Dr Kim and her husband are the founders of JBK Wellness Labs – an award-winning formulator and manufacturer of luxury natural health and beauty products for leading brands carried in Credo, Sephora, Ulta and Bergdorf. Rooted in her lineage's medical heritage, her formulas unite ancient herbal wisdom with modern science to promote wellness of both mind and body.

Dr Kim lives in San Diego with her husband and their two sons, and continues to travel the world sharing her teachings on Eastern medicine, wellness and Living Meditation.

To learn more about the author, please scan the QR code below.

@drjenellemkim

@drjenellekim